Alive With God

A Guide to Greater Faith

Rev. Paul Liston

LIGUORI PUBLICATIONS
One Liguori Drive
Liguori, Mo. 63057

Imprimi Potest:
Edmund T. Langton, C.SS.R.
Provincial, St. Louis Province
Redemptorist Fathers

Imprimatur:
St. Louis, February 14, 1978
+ John N. Wurm
Vicar General of St. Louis

ISBN 0-89243-078-8

Library of Congress Catalog Card Number: 78-54157

All photos except cover by Wallowitch

Table of Contents

"Divine Providence is leading us toward a new order in human relationships, which, through the agency of men and, what is more, above and beyond their own expectations, are tending toward the fulfillment of higher and, as yet, mysterious and unforeseen designs."

— Pope John XXIII,
Address at the Opening
of the Second Vatican Council

FOREWORD

As a priest in campus ministry and parish life, I have met so many Catholics who draw upon a simple faith, who are not impelled by a mature appreciation of the glad tidings. They have an adult approach to secular pursuits, even quite professional skills in many areas, except at the very center of their being. This syndrome characterizes passive Catholics who walk with a spiritual limp and whisper the Good News with a lisp. Simple faith is not to be disparaged, but there is a fullness of faith to which we are called. God beckons us to move from simple faith to full faith.

Without any pretensions of completeness, this overview of the Catholic faith touches only upon salient themes which seem to need refurbishing. Here is the old and new which the Christian householder should be able to bring forth from his storeroom.

Thanks are due to Charlotte Fletcher, my secretary, Sister Agnes Vincent Rueshoff, Karin Thornton, and to all who aided by their editorial advice and sustaining encouragement. I also extend gratitude to *The Catholic Standard* of the Washington, D.C., Archdiocese for permission to reprint portions of Chapter II which originally appeared in that newspaper.

As did St. Paul, I hope that "you will be able to grasp fully, with all the holy ones, the breadth and length and height and depth of Christ's love, and experience this love which surpasses all knowledge, so that you may attain to the fullness of God himself" (Eph 3:18-19).

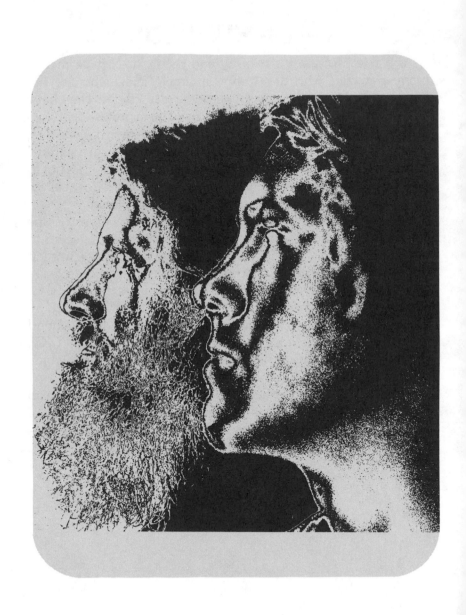

I
God:
Alive, Mysterious, Fascinating

The science fiction film *2001* focuses repeatedly on a black slab that appears on the landscape, compelling a sense of mystery and awe. It is evidently a symbol of some superhuman power. Often enough we may think of our God in terms of some such monumental black rock, looming large and inert. If anything, this may be the worst possible analogy for a God who is very much alive and well — the "living God" who communicates life as his best gift. A stone slab may be an apt image of a dead or impotent God, but not of the Lord God of Israel who is alive and on the move.

Jeremiah (Chapter 10) derides the folly of thinking of God as inanimate. He speaks of the pagan idols who are "dumb and senseless . . . without breath of life." By contrast, he says, "The Lord is true God, he is the living God." We might well examine our own God to see whether he is vitally alive. Perhaps in our minds we have erected an immobile stone slab planted grotesquely in the landscape, something grown too immense to be lively or nimble. The folk song entitled "Lord of the Dance" better mirrors our God who is quite dynamic and energetic, doing things and making things happen.

The first great lesson of the Bible is that there is only one God. And he is unique precisely because he is alive and brings things to life. He is creative and on-moving in contrast to the powerless dead gods who, as Jeremiah quips, "must be carried about." Nobody has to carry our God around; he is always far ahead beckoning us to catch up!

Our God Is Different

We relate better to the living than we do to inanimate objects. A prize specimen rock enshrined in a display case has little or nothing to do with relationship; we merely possess it. But to encounter anything living is to enter into give-and-take, surprise, deepening awareness, feedback, and all those aspects that make living relationships fascinating. Anything alive has the power to intrigue us. Encounter with the living leads to mystery.

One of the easiest ways to assure a best-selling book is to write a good mystery story. (For that matter, every story is a mystery — a "What happened next?") Mystery involves us as no other form can. Yet, to assert that God is alive and therefore mysterious somehow turns people off. They feel that calling God mysterious somehow avoids or evades their questions. On the contrary, we should expect that the story of God would be especially mysterious and, thus, all the more spellbinding. Who wants a God who is like anyone else! Our God is different; he has mystique (maybe "mystique" is less threatening than "mystery"). His is the kind of mystique that elicits the remark: "I like you. You're different!"

We are always off on the wrong foot when we try to appraise God as we judge anyone else. We cannot "psyche" God out — he is a mystery wrapped in a mystery. Another great teaching of the Old Testament, one we have yet to learn, is "My ways are not your ways." Pride of intellect may be our besetting sin, the same overbearing confidence as Job had in his own ability to solve the mystery of God. Job's dilemma is not resolved until he acknowledges:

I have dealt with great things that I do not understand; things too wonderful for me, which I cannot know (Job 42:3).

As the poster slogan proclaims: "God is a mystery to be enjoyed, not a problem to be solved." Rather than a riddle which alienates us, God should be a mystery that fascinates and beckons. This is the sort of intrigue in which St. Paul glories when he says, "How deep are the richness and the wisdom and the knowledge of God! How inscrutable his judgments, how unsearchable his ways! . . . To him be glory forever." This is not a God who is boring — because he does only the expected. This is one relationship we cannot box into the narrow confines of our expectations. Our God is different and delightfully so! He delights in surprise and wonder.

God of the Improbable

The truth wrapped in surprise and wonder we call a "paradox." This kind of apparent contradiction has been nicely described by Chesterton as "the truth standing on its head." God, for instance, chooses the weak things of this world to confound the strong, the so-called foolish to outwit the wise, the lowly he seats ahead of the mighty.

By secular standards his value system is strange, to say the least. It was not at all "odd of God to choose the Jews" — it was quite characteristic of him. And the Incarnation of God we see in Jesus pursues this same irony. The very name "Jesus of Nazareth" is a bundle of contradictions; after all, "What good can come out of Nazareth?" Jesus, as Israel found, was a Messiah of a very different stripe. His teaching of the last and the least occupying the first places puzzled many (it is entirely contrary to protocol). The doctrine "Sell what you have and give to the poor" so as to have heavenly treasure is unsound and unorthodox economic policy. The ultimate paradox of dying to oneself so as to find life was just too much for many of Jesus' followers to take. Yet, this is the revelation of God we have, a God of the improbable who sets out to prove that "what is impossible with men, is possible with God."

Since our God most assuredly delights in the unexpected and the unlikely, it means that he can be delight-full only to those who appreciate his sense of ironic humor. Anyone who wants to be in touch with, on the same wavelength with this creative, living God has to let go of the conventional values that prize power, profits, and pride of intellect. The only way to be friends with someone so highly unconventional is to relax and enjoy his unique humor.

Paul of Tarsus was such a man. He appreciated God's "foolishness" and became a "Fool for Christ's sake." His keen sense of God's reverse English was only reinforced when he debated the philosophers of Athens, using their own worldly wisdom for a change, and failing miserably. Secular "savvy," as he found, has so few answers to the really important questions. Like Job, we too must learn that "getting smart" is realizing that we know so little of the great things of God. Wisdom is knowing that God much prefers the weak and the powerless and enjoys doing the impossible for them. It was the little child (a powerless nonentity in Jewish law) who was pushed forward as the unlikely Christian model. Only in this way can God's power and God's agency be manifest. Very often episodes of the Old Testament are concluded with a "thus, you will know that it is the Lord God who has done this." He ordains the unexpected just to prove that it is his power and not our strategy that counts.

God Is a Community

After saying that God is alive, as well as mysterious and unconventional, we might be stimulated to get to know him a bit better. The former TV show *Person To Person* took us into the homes of notables to see for ourselves just how they lived. If our God is lively with a mind of his own, we might be curious about his life style at home. Just how does he live, what is his interior home style like? The New Testament Scriptures especially give us such a person-to-person view of God at home with himself. But remember now, we look with the notion in mind that God is different, and expectedly so.

A child once asked whether God was lonely. Actually this is a very perceptive question that strikes at the very core of the divine life. The Bible tells us that God is not at all lonely; what's more, he is a community complete within himself. We ourselves crave community; we want to belong. We judge solitary confinement the worst of punishments. But there is no fear that God is isolated or restricted to the life of a hermit. God within himself is a cycle of relationships we could only aptly call a complete community. This singular and unique Lord of all lives so richly that one person would not be enough to contain him. The "Mystery of the Trinity" is simply the truth that God at home lives well and to the full.

If, as St. Paul comments, we now see through a dark glass, that is especially true when considering the person-to-person inner life of God. The Trinity is where God ticks, so to speak, and might presumably be *the* great thing of God that we would not understand. We don't even comprehend our own inner life; so God's mainspring would necessarily be obscured from us. That, however, should not stop us from peeking and speculating. Such a glance can only fascinate while it yet puzzles.

God Is Truth and Love

The Greek philosophers were master speculators. One of them, Plotinus, nicely reasoned that one person only would not be enough to fulfill a perfect God. Plotinus speculated that an intellectually alive God would so well understand and reflect on himself that his thought would be not merely "something on his mind," but Someone. God thinks so richly and completely that he perfectly images himself. If God, say, were looking into a mirror, his reflection would be not merely a flat, inert likeness, but the true three-dimensional God looking back at himself. It would be a veritable likeness. In human language, anyone who fully embodies and reflects himself in another we call a "father"; the one so reflected and expressed we call a "son." (We might call the Father "God Understanding" and the Son "God Understood.")

Now we can hardly imagine, so to speak, that these two persons simply stare at one another without relating well. No, the wealth of communication between this Father and Son is such that we call it love. When two people are in love we customarily say that "there is something between them." Yet, when God loves so perfectly, it is not just "something" going on, it is a love so rich and full-blown that it is "Someone." This LOVE of God we call the Spirit of Holiness (Holy Spirit).

Do not try to subordinate the Son and the Spirit to the Father, saying "first there was the Father and afterward the Son and then the Spirit . . . ." We cannot apply the condition of time; the Trinity is an eternal cycle relationship. Nor do we try to divide God into three segments like a pie, asserting that the whole God is the sum of its parts. No, each person is fully divine; they are not like partial shareholders in a corporation. And even while saying all this, we believe that "God is one" (although complex in personality).

The creed of the Catholic faith affirms that there is "one God in three persons." It sounds improbable, but that is because we have met no human beings at all like this. And there is no one else quite like this! We cannot, though, limit reality to our meager experience. The Trinity is not a contradiction, for it looks at God from two distinct points of view. From one side we ask: "What is God?" "What is God's nature?" And we hear the answer (affirmed with us by both Judaism and Islam), "God is one." Then, from an entirely different standpoint, we pose another question: "Who is

God?" "What is his personality like?" "Is he lonely?" And the answer resounds, "God is not lonely!" This singular God lives such a rich and full life that he is a complete community in himself. This one God is three persons.

For all our speculation, do not think for a moment that we have solved or explained God. We have barely peeked into his person-to-person home life. What we see *should* mystify and yet attract us. We see a dynamic nature and an economy of persons that tell us that there is more to life than we realize. The Trinity tells us that there is a LIFE that is more satisfying and self-sustaining than our own. It tells us that there is a godly community where knowing and loving is an essential way of life — a wellspring of life that beckons to us. So let us stop agonizing over the mysterious Trinity and let us start enjoying it.

Our God Has It All Together

Having examined God part by part, let us put him back together again. In fact, there is no one quite as together as our God. We perceive various facets of the God-life; let us not forget that God is whole. He is whole because he works together beautifully; he is simplicity, economy itself. And there is a wholesomeness that also stems from God's being authentic, being simply what he is — "for real." We are so subject to image-making, fraudulent packaging, hypocrisy, and self-deception that anything or anyone real comes as a welcome surprise. We ourselves may hesitate to be authentic; and anyone who dares to be open and genuine compels our admiration.

Our God is Yahweh, the deity who "is what he is." There is no fudging, no posing. He is sheer integrity. He simply IS. As the Shaker hymn tune has it, "'Tis the gift to come down where we ought to be." And that's exactly where God is. To say that he is whole is simply another way of saying that he is holy. What's more, God is wholesome to the superlative degree — "Holy, holy, holy." He is wholly removed from deceit of any kind. He does not fear to be himself, even though that self is different. God is really himself "where he ought to be."

The Christian call "to be holy as your heavenly Father is holy" is not an enticement to play God, but a challenge to be our real selves. This wholeness characterizes the pure of heart ("single-hearted" is the better translation) blessed in Jesus' Sermon on the Mount. Rather than arbitrary hoops for mankind to jump through, the commandments are signposts for the integral human life. These guidelines given by this Holy One of Israel are a call to be authentically the reasoning, social, whole creature God so well designed. They are the manufacturer's working directions for being oneself. We too are invited to adopt the name Yahweh, "I am what I am," and so share the wholeness of the One-who-has-it-all-together.

To give a character sketch of the God who is distinctly different is a classic instance of speaking the "great things which I do not understand." Granted, our comprehension is limited and our insight is clouded. Fortunately, this God who knows himself and is himself has chosen to reach out to us in communication. And, as we shall see, he is his own message. He has revealed himself and even now still communicates with us. Maybe we are listening more to outer space than we are to the inner Spirit. For those who have open ears to hear and open eyes to see, there is the invitation and the promise that we may see him in all his difference, as he is, face-to-face, person-to-person. What "eye has not seen, ear has not heard, nor has it so much as dawned on man . . . God has prepared for those who love him" (1 Cor 2:9). It seems, then, that this God on the move is moving in our direction.

II
God:
Caring, Acting,
Communicating

If God is a complete community, then he really has no need of anyone else. Yet, we cannot accuse him of a Narcissus complex; he is not so captivated by his own image that he spends eternity simply admiring his reflection. He does seem somehow compelled to reach out beyond himself — he chooses to communicate, to be creative and involved. Ours is a living God on the move. He moves out and touches others, so potent is the force of his love. This kind of gregarious personality we call altruistic — other centered. But what is so incredible is the degree to which this God has gone. Not satisfied with mere revelation of himself, he has become engrossed in our affairs, and even immerses us in *his* affairs. Unlike a pompous monarch who merely makes pronouncements, our God sends out invitations, welcomes dialogue, and risks rejection. We are only beginning to appreciate how completely he has communicated himself. This kind of thoroughgoing communication we can rightly call "communion."

Notice that it is God who starts the dialogue. The Lord unfolds himself to us, not the other way around. God initiates and chooses; he reveals and challenges. As the Lord addressed Job, "I will question you and you tell me the answers!" We can only respond to the invitation or reject his overtures. Like it or not, every divine revelation poses a question which hangs there waiting for a responsive answer.

The Very Stones Cry Out

Communiqués from the Lord are varied in style. Some are as commonplace as everything natural and human around us. Paul tells the Christian community at Rome: "Since the creation of the world, invisible realities, God's eternal power and divinity, have become visible, recognized through the things he has made" (Rom 1:20). God obviously leaves his fingerprints on anything he creates. Everything from the simple beauty of a dandelion to the awesome immensity of nebulae tells of both his creative genius and his artistic skill. And yet he is something more than just an absentee landlord:

When I behold your heavens, the work of your fingers,
the moon and the stars which you set in place —

What is man that you should be mindful of him,
   or the son of man that you should care for him?
You have made him little less than the angels,
   and crowned him with glory and honor (Psalm 8).

We cannot forget that we too are part of creation's landscape and are ourselves telltale clues to the Creator. Coming to know ourselves and others gives telling information about the hand that molded us.

Truly you have formed my inmost being;
   you knit me in my mother's womb.
I give you thanks that I am fearfully, wonderfully made;
   wonderful are your works (Psalm 139).

A Break Through the Language Barrier

Aside from the natural clues we have, there is a beyond-the-natural revelation by God. In certain instances, God has broken through the normal course of human events. After all, physical nature and human nature can only convey so much about God, especially a God who is different. Wouldn't he have to educate us in special ways if we are to esteem his differences? Such "special education" he has undertaken. We are ordinarily taught through other men; this then would be the pattern God followed in our graduate education.

Such beyond-the-natural communication sooner or later encounters a language problem (not God's, but ours). God wishes to speak to men, but how? Since the language barrier is on our side, God, as it were, would have to learn our language. He condescends to speak in human tongues, and for that purpose he will literally employ a human tongue. God tapped Abraham, Moses, and others on the shoulder to speak for him; or rather, he spoke and acted through these men. As St. Paul later describes it, "God spoke in fragmentary and varied ways to our fathers through the prophets" (Heb 1:1).

The prophets were primarily preachers (and secondarily writers) inspired by God to be channels of his message — usually a call to a more righteous way of life. Contrary to popular notion, prophecy did not necessarily entail the foretelling of future events; in some cases it did, but usually the prophets were impelled to give what

Southerners would call "some mighty powerful preaching." (Although God often used women to champion his cause, the role of Old Testament prophet is apparently a male preserve. Later, however, the Acts of the Apostles speaks of Christian women who had the gift of prophecy.)

Prophets are said to be "inspired" because God's Spirit prompts and empowers them. The early notion of "spirit" in Jewish scriptures connotes power. When God's Spirit came upon a man he was empowered and moved to fulfill his mission. St. Augustine saw the prophets' inspiration as "the Spirit of God speaking with their lips." And the prophets had a lively sense of their gift; it was God's doing, his word. Usually a prophetic message is prefaced by "The Lord said to me" or "Thus says the Lord." Then it is delivered in the first person singular — a direct communiqué.

In Sure and Varied Ways

For all this, we must nevertheless admit that we do not know precisely how God's inspiration works. Let us just say that the patriarch or prophet was somehow stirred to say or write just what God wanted. In the process of inspiration God accommodates himself to the language, style, and life experience of the persons chosen. The prophet Amos, for example, speaks like the blunt shepherd-farmer he is, drawing on instances from the farmyard and field. He depicts locusts swarming on the late growth, or the Lord planting his people Israel in their own field. Candid and economical of speech, he is the Near Eastern equivalent of a Maine farmer. God thus uses people, without depriving them of their natural qualities. He never coerces, he empowers.

In the course of time, some of these chosen men wrote down (or dictated to others) the word of the Lord which came to them. The collection of these communiqués which recounts God's hand in human affairs makes up the most unique book in the history of the world. It is a book unlike any other, for it is in origin the Word of God, not the mere word of man. This book, therefore, has a power and an unction that can only be described as unparalleled. Curiously enough, the singular impact of the Bible has been best described by the antireligious Jean Jacques Rousseau: "Peruse

23

the words of our philosophers with all their pomp of diction; how mean, how contemptible they are, compared with the Scriptures. Is it possible that a book at once so simple and so sublime should be merely the work of man?"

How then do we know it is in fact God's message? Many have tried to prove the godly character of the Bible; still, they have not absolutely demonstrated its divine authorship. The difficulty is that we cannot prove the supernatural by the natural — "Flesh begets flesh, spirit begets spirit." These are two vastly different worlds. The Bible calls not for the proof of credentials, but for the reply of experience. It calls not for the skepticism of the scientist, but for the open response of the reader. We can only point to the Bible's wisdom which sanctifies, its truth which liberates, its beauty which beckons. It speaks to the heart! This Word gives spirit and life. For hundreds of generations of Jews and Christians it has served as a map of life. It all depends *how* it is read. "Whoever comes to it in piety, faith, and humility, and with a determination to make progress in it, will assuredly find there and will eat the 'bread that comes down from heaven!' " (Pope Benedict XV, 1920)

Which Bible?

There is much curiosity and confusion about the differences between the Catholic and Protestant versions of the Scriptures. "Which Bible?" is a valid question. Generally there is common agreement about large portions of the Bible which include the major books of prime importance. The only area of divergence is in the Old Testament; there the Catholic Bible is thicker by the addition of seven works. In ancient times there were arguments between conservative and liberal Jews over the true worth of these seven texts, mostly because they were not originally written in classical Hebrew like the others. The early Christian community was mainly Greek-speaking and so followed a Greek translation of the Jewish Scriptures that included the debated books. The Catholic Church still considers them inspired by God. Later, when Protestant communities came into being, they chose to follow the Jewish listing which did not include these seven books. Actually, the seven disputed portions of the Old Testament (the books of Tobit, Judith, Wisdom, Sirach, Baruch, 1 and 2 Maccabees, together with parts of Daniel) embody some of the more attractive Scripture readings.

Today, this gap between the two traditions has generally been resolved. Some Protestant versions include the seven works as "recommended reading" (revered, but not inspired). There are also cooperative efforts in translations. Catholic, Protestant, and Orthodox scholars have given us the so-called Common Bible. Thus, there are differences, but not of great practical moment. Even in Catholic circles there are various translations that have their own fans, for example, *The Jerusalem Bible,* the Ronald Knox translation, and *The New American Bible.* The Church has nothing to fear from any version of the Scriptures that is as faithful to the original as it can be. For that matter, comparing translations often helps our understanding of the text.

Truth of the Bible

By a process known perhaps only to himself, God wrote the Bible. Therefore, we can say that the Scriptures, like God himself, are true. But these truths take on many shapes. There is such a mixture of styles and forms in the Bible! Its contents range all the way from law to poetry, from kitchen recipes to proverbs, from history to fiction. Yes, fiction. The parables that Jesus told were fictional, but they had a truth to tell. Poetry, like the Psalms, uses fictitious exaggeration; yet, poetry can be a well for the deepest truth. Still other forms of Bible literature are quite alien to us, like John's Book of Revelation. All of which points up the fact that the Bible is a quite varied and complex work, the truth of which is not always as obvious as we might expect. For all this, there are basic truths open and available for all.

Contrary to popular belief, the Catholic Church has not defined the meaning of every Scripture verse. In actual fact, there are only a few brief passages of Scripture that the Church has determined in this way. Generally, a Catholic is free, if he so wishes, to be a fundamentalist (a believer in the *literal* meaning of the Bible, for example, that God performed the acts of creation in a week of seven days of twenty-four hours). A Catholic is likewise just as free to seek the truth of a passage as it comes in the context of its form (history or poetry), the intent of the writer, the culture and customs of the time, or the limits of the language. For instance, we have already referred to the Old Testament notion of "spirit" as "power." This derives from the customary use of the language at the time, as well as from the religious culture a Jew brought with him to the synagogue. Their understanding of a given word was quite different from what our own culture means by the same word. We are free, then, to be fundamentalists if we will. However, it does seem a shame to neglect the vast scholarship and discoveries of this last century. What with the recent disclosures of the Dead Sea Scrolls and the like, we know so much better how to reach into the Bible for God's truth. Beyond asking "What did God say?" we should be asking "What did God mean?"

In reading God's Word for ourselves we not only have the same Spirit which inspired its wisdom, we also have the very Church which wrote it. The Book of the Bible is not suspended in midair, but is held in the hand of God's community, whose word it is. True, God wrote the Scriptures, but he did so using various individuals. This community of the Church first spoke and preached God's message before it ever committed it to writing. It was the end of the first Christian century (about 90 A.D.) before John put down his pen after writing the last word of the last book of the Bible. Thus, the Christian community (the Church) existed some two or three generations before the Bible was even finished. It is her book then. As Bishop Sheen nicely phrases it, "The Bible came out of the Church, not the Church out of the Bible."

The Bible is not an encyclopedia of religious thought. In the New Testament, for example, the Gospel of Matthew and the Letters of Paul were each written for very specific reasons. Even John himself professes that "Jesus performed many other signs as well — signs not recorded here — in the presence of his disciples. But these have been recorded to help you believe . . ." (Jn 20:30-31). As profound as it is, this holy book is not the totality of God's self-revelation. This God on the move cannot be bound and locked between two book covers. In the course of time even our understanding of the old text continues to find new depth of meaning under the guidance of the same Spirit who wrote it. As we shall find, God continues reaching out to people in varied ways. The Bible is, however, our greatest written witness to "God in search of man."

Reading Today's Good News

The reading of any book is conditioned by the attitude we bring to it. The beauty and excitement of the Bible are likewise in the beholder. As God inspired the text, so he also enlightens the reader — at least the reader who is open to the idea that God's Spirit still empowers. God speaks to the heart of the humble, those who open the Scriptures with a prayer: "Lord, take out my heart of stone and give me a heart of flesh."

That the Gospel is "good news" literally headlines Mark's contribution to the Bible — from his very opening verse. There is the excitement of tabloid events which "amazed all those who looked on." Yet, one of the truisms of journalism is that nothing is as old as yesterday's newspaper. Just so, the good news of the Bible is in danger of becoming simply yesterday's old news. We tend to lose something of the excitement and amazement of the people who witnessed the original Biblical events. The Bible was purposely written to make salvation present and active, not just to relate past events. And it still has this power to re-present rather than simply to remember God's saving acts. The Old Testament readers never understood God's Word as an ineffectual voice crying in a bygone wilderness, but as possessing power in the present. As they saw it, when Yahweh speaks, things happen. The same Word power can leap out to us from the pages of the Bible if we so read them, expecting Spirit and Life. The contemporary New Testament translation *Good News for Modern Man* is aptly titled since God's Word has a life-giving power to this day; it is still today's headlines.

If you are searching for a text to *put excitement back into your Bible reading,* why not read Tobit as witness of what God did and continues to do for his people? On why not reread the Gospel of Mark as today's sensational news with the same sort of drama and excitement which the headliner John the Baptizer generated? Mark highlights John the Baptizer; no such prophet had spoken by

God's direction for over five hundred years. The silence of five centuries had been broken, the fullness of time had come! With a flurry, "All the Judean countryside and the people of Jerusalem went out to him in great numbers" (Mk 1:5). Now that's a headline! Mark's is the earliest of the Gospel accounts — hot off the presses, and should be read as such. Some scholars now think that scarcely thirty years after Christ's death Mark, in a kind of white heat, took pen in hand. Thus, Mark's Gospel is the freshest account, containing in bold relief many concrete details which are obscured in the later evangelists.

To look on the Bible as a kind of Dead Sea Scroll merely recounting nostalgic, bygone history is to misread God's Word. Ours is a God of the living, not of the dead. His Word of good news is still very much a "NOW" event.

III
Trouble
in Eden

A book-length exposé of suburban housing developments some years back had the apt title, *A Crack in the Picture Window*. From our own experience we are forced to admit that human nature, indeed the whole world setting we inhabit, is an ideal that has somehow become flawed. We have only to look about us or read the morning paper! We see a disjointed world: man at odds with himself, at enmity with his fellow-man, man the enemy of nature, an outcast from his very Maker. St. Paul traced his finger along this crack in the window when he observed, with some frustration, "I cannot even understand my own actions. I do not do what I want to do but what I hate" (Rom 7:15). All this does make us wonder what went wrong! We cannot blame it on the oven door slamming by chance in the baking process. Something more radical and deep-reaching surely flawed the better plan God had envisioned. Cardinal Newman infers "some terrible aboriginal calamity." Karl Marx in *Das Kapital* flatly asserts that "original sin is at work everywhere." We might well ask about God's better idea, "What went wrong?" Or more precisely, "Who is to blame?"

The Genesis story is not only a simple yet effective account of creation's great truths but also the satisfying solution to the mystery of the broken window. The family of man simply failed or refused to live up to its part in the cosmic plan. Call it irresponsibility if you will, the failure to respond appropriately. It is the old story of a creation which, in a Frankenstein manner, turns on its master. And this is not just Adam's failure to respond; we have all done our own personal share of window breaking. Whether it be the so-called original sin or our own moral shortcomings is beside the point. We are the villains of the play, we have together shattered God's good plan. And so we all experience alienation at every level of life because we, together with others, have chosen to play out a plot of our own making. Our own scheme of things was better, so we thought . . . .

A Special Relationship

What is the truth of the Genesis story of creation? The story form and its details, it would seem, are a way of pointing up certain basic truths. It says that God is the Creator of ALL things, be they the natural features of earth, or sea life, or insects and animals, or mankind itself. If they take their existence from God, then he, and not his handiwork, is to be worshiped — given prime credit and priority. In contrast with the pagan religions and their litanies of material and human deities, Genesis focuses upon the single Lord of ALL, who alone is "the Holy One, the Great One." He alone is worth the free offering of ourselves in awe and gratitude. As Jesus tells Martha, "One thing only is required."

The Genesis account also highlights man and woman as a special creation of the Maker, his masterpiece. They are made in God's image and likeness; they "walk with him in the cool of the day"; they are given stewardship over all the other elements in the grand design. Eden's harmony between man and nature was the order of the day, in stark contrast with the imbalance and misuse of nature we now encounter. There were no killer bees then — nature was beneficent. (Ecology happily emerges now as man's use of nature in harmony with the grand design.) Man was indeed the apple of God's eye, surrounded as he was by "various trees . . . that were delightful to look at and good for food." It was the original ideal housing development! Somebody up there obviously liked mankind.

The tragic truth of the creation's story is man's breach of that special relationship. Godlike, we went our own way, only to find how dependent, how impoverished we really were. The serpent told a half truth: We did not become like God, but we certainly did come to know good and evil.

Apples and Serpents

Surely "What was the original sin?" has been the topic of speculation ever since the first telling of the epic of Eden. Yet, we must get beyond the notion of apples and serpents and arbitrary hurdles thrown up by a capricious Creator; there is certainly more at stake here than eating or not eating the fruit of a certain tree. The chaos around us derives from deeper roots.

Perhaps the dialogue of the serpent in the Genesis story gives us a hint of what cracked the picture window. Of the forbidden fruit the serpent asserts that "the moment you eat of it you will be like gods, who know what is good and what is bad." This is the classic enticement to worship ourselves rather than God, to deify self rather than adore. Isn't this the perennial temptation — to be more than we are, to refuse to be the integral, genuine self we are before God? We hear an echo of this self-deception in the enticement by Shakespeare's Lady Macbeth: she assures Macbeth that if he kills Duncan, he could be "so much more the man!" Macbeth's over-reaching himself is the tragic axis on which the play turns. It just might be that the first sin is very like the last, and all those in-between. As the Victorians phrased it, we simply do not know our place.

There is no doubt about it; we are the progeny of the first humans. The old lure speaks right to us since we too are so unready to be ourselves in God's scheme of things. Not content to be like God in his image, we strive to be God; we want to be all-knowing and all-powerful, self-sufficient and self-sustaining. To someone so "puffed up" (as Paul describes it), one could retort, "Have you ever had a group picture taken of yourself?" In Genesis and ever around us, we witness this arrogance of arrogation, which, as the dictionary defines it, is "to assume or claim something as one's own, unduly, proudly, and presumptuously." Adam and Eve were playing God; and their game still has its avid fans. It is interesting that the faith of Islam is especially sensitive to this besetting game; the very name "Islam" means "submission."

Weeds in the Wheat

Once man starts to go his own route disaster strikes. Adam puts the blame on Eve, and Eve blames the serpent. Already the fabric of an orderly society is torn. Pandora's box is open! To step out of right relationship with one's Maker means being at odds with all levels of creation, be it with nature, with one's fellow-man, or with oneself. The weeds in the wheat, our poverty in truly relating to one another, the nightmare of cancer, the darkness of death — "all the ills flesh is heir to" — stem from alienating ourselves from the Master's better plan. And perhaps "alienation" is the most apt word to describe our exile from God.

Did you ever see the famous old motion-picture film of a California suspension bridge that collapsed very shortly after it was erected in the '30s? You watch this news film in fascination and horror as the grand bridge structure sways madly and then completely collapses. That's the way it was between God and man; the bridge of special relationship came tumbling down!

East of Eden

Where does this leave the human story? Is it a hopeless tragedy? Must man inexorably live out his choices? In all justice this might well have been; for if man would walk away, God would let him. But no, East of Eden was not to be a permanent address. Along with the consequences of rebellion, the creation story likewise tells of a promise and a hope. There is a mysterious hint of daybreak to come: God says to the serpent, "I will put enmity between you and the woman, and between your offspring and hers; he will strike at your head, while you strike at his heel" (Gn 3:15). There will be continued warfare between mankind and the forces of evil, but there will also be an eventual victory over evil. The punishments are not eternal, but remedial. Like Emily Dickenson's bird of hope, there awaits the dawn of a new creation:

Hope is a thing with feathers
  That perches in the soul
And sings the tune without words,
  And never stops at all
And sweetest in the gale is heard.

Considering the force of the gale, this hope promises nothing less than a new creation. And anyone who lives by the Scriptures, be he Jew or Christian, embodies that hope. Essentially both are an optimistic people who trust that God will write another "Book of Beginnings," a second Genesis.

The Old Testament, the story of the "People of the Promise" as the Jews called themselves, is a commentary on the sort of God who binds himself to such promises, who holds out such a hope. It would not be an exaggeration to call him soft-hearted. Like a typical father, God is partial — even indulgent — to his offspring. The acid test of divine love comes when the one loved is totally undeserving because he has been totally unresponsive. Thus, it is not our charm or merit that captivates God, but his love which constantly radiates an inviting warmth, often despite our unresponsiveness. Ours is not a fair-weather God; the same altruistic love that first initiated a special relationship just keeps on welcoming. God tries not to lose his friends. (He is hardly the sort of companion who picks up his marbles and walks off in a huff.) The Psalms especially praise God's "constant love," by which they mean a truly insistent and relentless regard, even in the face of faint return. This is what the Bible means by perfect love — a love like God's own which never gives up! Jesus challenges those who follow in his steps to love in this way — even the unworthy. This is the miracle of the Christian life!

If you love those who love you, what credit is that to you? Even sinners love those who love them (Lk 6:32).

This may not be good business management, but it is authentic love. The basic premise of Christianity is the realization that we are loved precisely in this way.

A New Creation

And so the Creator goes back to the drawing board. His insistent love will occasion nothing short of a thoroughgoing re-creation. "Lo, I am about to create new heavens and a new earth" (Is 65:17). Now, beyond communicating himself, there is also the additional concern for atonement and reconciliation. We find it difficult to talk to someone with his back turned to us. First, we have to get his attention, that is, turn him around before we can engage in true dialogue. If the bridge between God and man is down, there is no getting around the fact that another more serviceable structure must be built, another more direct line of communication strung.

The essential requirement for any bridge is that it have one pier on either shore — to bridge gaps or differences we simply must have one foot on either side. And this is precisely what this relentless, loving God designed. He would join the community across the gap and thus gain a sure foothold in their midst. He would learn their language by total immersion; among them he would even "learn obedience by suffering." The preface to John's Gospel gives the most succinct description of this plan — "The Word became flesh and made his dwelling among us." (The Hebrew sense is "He pitched his tent in our midst.") One of God's persons (the Son, God's very Image and Word who accurately re-presents him, of course) would completely bridge himself over so that we might, in turn, be transported back to the Father. "God so loved the world that he gave his only Son, that whoever believes in him may not die but may have eternal life. God did not send the Son into the world to condemn the world, but that the world might be saved through him" (Jn 3:16-17). Now when John speaks of "eternal life" he means God's way of living, God's family life that we can genuinely share. This gift is not the *everlasting* prolongation of human life, but a participation in God's own *eternal* life. God makes his home with us that he might bring us home; God historically joins the family of man so that we might join the family of God. Now, is there any more special relationship than that? Anyone who responds to and accepts the Father's embodied message, his Word, "he empowered to become children of God."

IV

Covenant: The Never-ending Love Story

If God is going to reconcile the human race to himself, if he is going to build a real bridge and not just a rainbow in the sky, then he will literally have to "pitch his tent in our midst." If we are to be at home with God, then God will have to be at home with us. More is required than simply sending a man, or appearing as a man; God must *be* a man! There can be no "let's pretend." Dorothy Day makes the point that for love to be experienced it has to be real: "Love must become incarnate."

The basic requirement for membership in the human race is actual conception, followed by birth. In reaching out to us, God would even go so far as to be "knit in a mother's womb," as the Psalm describes it. So compelling is the force of his love that he would undergo this initiation into the human family, with all its consequences. True love demands complete sharing. They say that an Irish marriage proposal goes something like "How would you like to be buried with my people?" Yes, that kind of sharing. As Ruth says to her mother-in-law Naomi, "Wherever you lodge I will lodge. . . . Wherever you die I will die, and there be buried" (1:16-17). Now that's involvement for you! God does "marry up" with the human race, for so the Old Testament often speaks of it.

Catholics in the past have often given short shrift to the Old Covenant portion of the Bible; we skimmed over the initial story of the sometimes uneasy marriage and went on to the birth announcement. Happily that is now changing. We cannot know where we are or where God is leading us without knowing where we have been. The Old Testament is the family history of any Jew or Christian. Much more than mere nostalgia, it contains our spiritual genes; it is our genesis. For that matter, the Christian portion of the Scriptures much concerns itself with ancestral roots: Matthew begins his Gospel, "This is the family record of Jesus Christ, who was a descendant of David, who was a descendant of Abraham." As we all come to learn early in life, being human involves a web of family relationships, a whole trunkful of ancestors, some of whom may not be all that savory. (You do not have to dig deeply at all to find the skeletons in Jesus' family closet!) And so it was with the marriage of Yahweh and Israel.

God's Tribe

It cannot be said that God's engineering for human reconditioning (call it building bridges and pitching tents, if you will) was anything but thorough. His re-creative plan starts by selecting and molding an entire tribal nation of his own to be known as "the People of God." In a kind of second genesis, in his usual improbable way, the Lord took the most commonplace, elemental folk and fashioned them into his own unique tribe. (Occasionally Yahweh has to remind them that they were "nobodies" before he chose them.) Thus, the Bridge Builder to come would have family roots going back some 2,000 years of recorded history. There were many lessons to be learned by the tribe in their geographic and spiritual wanderings, lessons best learned by long, sometimes painful, experience. It would take at least that much time to comprehend the implications of God's saving plan. They would have to appreciate the fact that, as Ezekiel explains, God himself would shepherd and feed his flock. They must learn that the Lord's love in their midst is more than some*thing* they could experience; it would be some*one* they could call cousin.

This formation and education of God's tribe began with Abram, a Semitic nomad-shepherd from Ur, the principal city of Chaldea. The divine call came to Abram: "Go forth from the land of your kinfolk and from your father's house to a land that I will show you. I will make of you a great nation, and I will bless you." In summoning Abram to come away from his previous life and kinships, this voice was asking nothing short of voluntary exile, which in those times meant dire alienation and probable death. In turn, Abram was given only the vague promise of a land yet to be seen, along with assurances of a blessing yet to be experienced. What is more, there was the grandiose promise that in him "all the communities of the earth shall find blessing." It is no wonder that St. Paul acclaims Abram as "the man of faith," approved because he risked all at the Lord's word. And thus, the reconciliation of the entire human family to God began with the risk-taking faith of a single Chaldean shepherd. Equipped with little more than a grandly changed name (Abraham, "Father of Nations"), he started his adventure in trust, very much as God's people of subsequent ages would entrust themselves into his care.

Abraham's venture, in the nature of a pilgrimage, leads him over difficult, foreign terrain to a new land. Many of the hazards Abraham meets are also rich encounters with his new Lord. Each difficult traverse along the pilgrim path becomes the site for a shrine remembering God's fidelity to his promises. In a pact that is still ongoing, we see the successful working out of a kind of feudal alliance between the shepherd nomad and his Lord God, continually reinforced by God's promise, "If you will be my people, I will be your God." So begins the serial adventures of God and his tribe, which, like most marriages, was both for better and worse.

The alliance, however, was conditional, "If you will be my people. . . ." The tribal members found themselves beneficiaries as long as they trusted their Lord and not themselves (which was not always the case). For his part, God was teaching and opening their eyes in readiness for "the Light to come." Readiness was the point of it all, for not only were they themselves to benefit from the marriage, but they were also to be the agents of blessing for all mankind. Sadly, there were times when much had to be unlearned, often by bitter experience.

The Journey Within

Without chronicling the entire history of Israel, let us just note a few of the insights the Jewish people discovered. For example, they found that they could not be half-hearted in the service of their generous Master; he could also be jealous and demanding. "To whom much is given, much is required." They could not serve other gods as well, or pay tithes and still price-gouge the poor. Also, it required more than periodic payments to keep their alliance in force — every day, every moment, was holy to the Lord. They further learned that they could not give their bodies to gestures of ritual service while not giving their hearts — he knows all, he reads hearts! It was incompatible to sing psalms and all the while lust after the neighbor's wife. "I want love and not sacrifice . . . (Hos 6:6). Rend your hearts and not your garments" (Joel 2:13).

The Old Testament progressively develops this theme of religious interiority, which is very much an ongoing concern of the Gospels. A right relationship with God is the pilgrimage within; the intent must mirror the act so that, like God, they are likewise whole, or "together." The Lord loves the single-hearted, the wholehearted ("pure of heart"), while he rejects the hypocrite. The most terrible disaster to beset Israel — the destruction of the Temple along with the enslavement by Babylon — raised the cry, "How could this happen to God's very own chosen people?" The painful answer, mulled over in captivity, was, "We have given our hands, but not our hearts." Unlike the pagan gods who were content with an occasional offering or whiff of incense, Yahweh required that total dedication called love, a faithful and all-consuming love like his own.

Yahweh Falls in Love

Much was required, but much was given. The relationship was not simply a compact with an overlord founded on threats and demands. No. The Lord gave choice land, the best of wheat and wine, security from enemies, many tokens of tender loving care. Yahweh nurtured Israel as his own:

. . . offspring of Abraham my friend — you whom I have taken from the ends of the earth and summoned from its far-off places, you whom I have called my servant, whom I have chosen and will not cast off — fear not, I am with you; be not dismayed; I am your God. I will strengthen you, and help you, and uphold you with my right hand of justice . . . . For I am the Lord, your God, who grasp your right hand; it is I who say to you, 'Fear not, I will help you.'' . . . I have called you by name; you are mine . . . . You are precious in my eyes and glorious . . . I love you (Is 41:8-10, 13; 43:1, 4).

The God of Israel is aptly described in Old Testament literature as the Good Shepherd, the Faithful Teacher, the Provident King — all very much the Father who knows how to give good gifts to his children. "The Lord withholds no good thing from those who walk in sincerity" (Psalm 84:12). He is "merciful and gracious, slow to anger, abounding in kindness and fidelity" (Psalm 86:15). Nothing could be farther from the truth than the simplistic myth that the God of the Old Covenant is one of stern justice, while the God of the New is loving and tender. (Read Isaiah, Chapters 43 and 44, to sample Yahweh's concern for his people after a lover's

46

quarrel.) The God of Abraham, Isaac, and Jacob, the God of Peter, James, and John is the same Lord who always "proclaims peace to his people . . . to those who put in him their hope." He is ever ready to forgive all, if they would only turn to him, repentant. Perhaps the saddest verse of the entire Bible is Jesus' lament: "O Jerusalem, Jerusalem . . . how often have I wanted to gather your children together as a mother bird collects her young under her wings, and you refused me!" (Luke 13:34)

The Inverted Pyramid

Among the lessons to be digested over the centuries by God's tribe was the notion that the salvation to come was not some*thing,* but some*one.* Evidently God gives some credence to the Shaker proverb: "If you want anything done, do it yourself." Along with gratefully remembering the Lord's favors, Israel awaited the One-who-is-to-come. The prophets reiterated the promise that this awaited Shepherd, Teacher, and King would lead and feed Israel, along with all the peoples of the earth.

The history of salvation (very much Jewish family history) is like an inverted pyramid, beginning on the broadest possible scene with the creation story and by degrees narrowing in focus to a single individual. This narrowing process progresses by rather curious selections and is even furthered unintentionally by unworthy individuals. What winnows out is a tattered but faithful remnant comprised mostly of the devout poor who have not given up hope in Yahweh's fidelity to his word. Some are impoverished descendants of the glorious King David, literally royalty on the rocks who "wait upon the Lord."

The narrowing of the salvation pyramid proceeds thus: from Abraham's son Isaac and his son Jacob descends the Hebrew nation. Then the blessing of the promise rests upon the Jewish tribe of Judah and later Judah's royal clan of David. The line next descends and narrows to a particular family, and then to a single individual. Oddly enough, God's choice lights upon a teen-age girl (13 or 14 years old perhaps) from Nazareth, a mean village in "unholy Galilee." From the standpoint of Oriental culture and law, this girl is a nonentity. Yet, the momentous burden of Israel's past and future (the inverted pyramid) bears down upon her! But then the God of Israel is like that — this teen-ager from Nazareth is the prime instance of God using the powerless to fulfill his power. Only God can build well on sand! (The Women's Liberation Movement has nothing to fear when it realizes that the broad scene of salvation history narrowed to a woman in a male-dominated society.)

At the Sharp Point

As it came to Abraham, the Word of God came to "a virgin betrothed to a man named Joseph, of the house of David. The virgin's name was Mary" (Lk 1:27). She too, like Abraham, was promised a blessing at the price of great risk. The Baby promised her would constitute both the blessing and the danger. God's message to her, which gives the long litany of titles for the Messiah (Great One, Son of God, King Forever, Holy One, etc.), clearly spelled out the blessing, a benediction Abraham would dearly love to have seen. Progeny, however, also had its perils in this instance, especially in a society which would not understand that this Child was God's and not someone else's. The penalty for suspected adultery could well have been death for Mary, as well as for Joseph who would be suspected of complicity. Jesus' conception in the face of Mary's virginity was God's problem, she may have thought, but she would have to face the neighbors.

Fortunately, Joseph the carpenter, the anxious and perplexed bridegroom, was not kept in the dark for long. He too had a role in this venture of trust, which was to give the Child a legal name and to round out the family setting. God's message to Joseph is perhaps the clearest Gospel statement of Mary's circumstance and God's intent:

Joseph, son of David, have no fear about taking Mary as your wife. It is by the Holy Spirit that she has conceived this child. She is to have a son and you are to name him Jesus because he will save his people from their sins (Mt 1:20-21).

Matthew the Evangelist sees here the clear application of Isaiah's puzzling prophecy: "The virgin shall be with child and give birth to a son, and they shall call him Emmanuel, a name which means 'God is with us' " (Mt 1:23).

God's Spirit is clearly life force enough to initiate the unfolding of human cells which would embody him among us. Yet, even here, God leans upon the acquiescence of a young girl. Mary's "yes," like Abraham's "yes," began her pilgrimage of reliance on the Lord. Yahweh's many promises to Abraham and his offspring were then literally fulfilled in her. As a consequence, Mary is not a goddess, but a human heroine. God's choice of Mary and her nod of assent makes her the most unique of ordinary mortals, for she is at the sharp thrust-point of salvation history.

V
Jesus
Identifies Himself

After preaching and healing elsewhere, Jesus returned to his hometown of Nazareth a celebrity. In the synagogue on the Sabbath, like any rabbi or Jew of note, he would be invited to read the assigned Scripture lesson and comment on its meaning. All eyes were fixed upon him, so Luke comments. The reading that Sabbath happened to be a passage from Isaiah.

The spirit of the Lord God is upon me, because the Lord has anointed me; he has sent me to bring glad tidings to the lowly, to heal the brokenhearted, to proclaim liberty to the captives and release to the prisoners, to announce a year of favor from the Lord . . . (Isaiah 61:1-2).

Jesus' homily on its meaning is the clearest assertion of his role as Messiah: "Today this Scripture passage is fulfilled in your hearing." In effect, he said, "This means me!"

The hometown audience was charmed by his rhetoric, yet puzzled and even annoyed by his sudden emergence as an able preacher and effective healer. His neighbors rather thought they knew everything there was to know about Jesus Ben Joseph. Somehow their stereotype did not fit the man standing present before them. Neighbors who "know it all" do not like having their cherished labels, their comfortable conventions shattered. And so it was that the self-disclosed Messiah "could work no miracle there . . . so much did their lack of faith distress him." The Gospels comment that "they found him too much for them." Indeed their discomposure turned to anger, so much so that they tried to throw Jesus off the chalk cliff on which Nazareth is built!

The fact is, the Nazarenes were having an identity crisis — Jesus' identity. They assumed that Joseph was the true father of Jesus, and yet the figure before them little spoke or acted like Joseph's son. "Where did this man get such wisdom and miraculous powers? Isn't this the carpenter's son?" The Gospels keep returning to this same question of Christ's identity. The apostles ask, "Who can this be that the wind and the sea obey him?" Even Jesus himself raises the question of his person in a pointed inquiry to his followers. These questions follow him to the grave: "Are you the Messiah, the Son of the Blessed One?" "Are you the King of the

Jews?" It is this same concern for Jesus' identity that confronts anyone who has ever heard the name. We still hear Jesus' question: "Who do you say that I am?"

"What Do You Have to Say for Yourself?"

Many different answers have been given to the query about Christ's identity. Some, like his own contemporaries, simply call him "Rabbi," meaning "Teacher"; others hail him as merely a messiah, or a religious genius, a prophet, a religious reformer, a political rebel, a guru, a healer, or a saint. Even the demons Jesus encounters have their own favorite title of address (curiously, the correct one). Appropriately, the more pertinent solution comes from Jesus' own lips. What did he have to say for himself? What are his own claims? And how did his audience hear him and understand his assertions?

Jesus himself lays claim to many titles. He formally acknowledges that he is the One-who-is-to-come, the awaited Priest-King who would rule for all ages (the Hebrew "Messiah" or the Greek "Christ"). Jesus readily admits this in the Nazareth synagogue, and later to his disciples and before Jerusalem officialdom at his trial. Jesus of Nazareth likewise accepts "Rabbi"; he is a religious genius, a prophet or preacher, a reformer and something of a rebel, a healer assuredly, and most certainly a holy man. Even guru perhaps! But is this all Jesus claims? He claims to be more than merely these. Jesus was murdered because he maintained that he was God! It was no crime in Jewish law to put oneself forward as Messiah, or healer and the like; there was only the burden of proof on the claimant. While Christ's criticism of the religious establishment was the likely motive, Jesus was tried and executed by his own people on the very specific charge of blasphemy — he said that Yahweh and he were one.

On one occasion (John, Chapter 10) Jesus encountered an audience so hostile that it took up stones to beat him to death. With a mastery of presence and some irony he asked, "Many good deeds have I shown you from the Father. For which of these do you stone me?" The answer from the mob was, "It is not for any 'good deed' that we are stoning you . . . but for blaspheming. You who are only a man are making yourself God." The accused goes on to ask further, "Do you claim that I blasphemed when . . . I said 'I am God's Son'? If I do not perform my Father's works, put no faith in me" (Jn 10:32-33, 36-37). Blasphemy of this sort is precisely the charge at Jesus' trial, for which the penalty was death.

The first three Gospel writers all detail the formal charges against the Nazarene and his interrogation before the highest court of Israel. What Jesus says in this official forum of his own people is of critical importance. Mark's Gospel is the earliest and clearest of the Bible witnesses to the trial proceedings:

> Once again the high priest interrogated him: 'Are you the Messiah, the Son of the Blessed One?' Then Jesus answered: 'I am; and you will see the Son of Man seated at the right hand of the Power and coming with the clouds of heaven.' At that the high priest tore his robes and said: 'What further need do we have of witnesses? You have heard the blasphemy' (Mark 14:61-64).

Three dignities are in contention here: Messiah, Son of the Blessed One (God), and Son of Man. Messiah he often said he was, but that declaration in court would not legally endanger him; Son of God and Son of Man would and did. Any Jew could claim Yahweh's paternal care by calling himself God's son. Far beyond that, it was evident to all who voted guilty that the defendant used the term in its unique sense as *the* Son of God. Mind you, he is asked to swear solemnly that he is "the Son of the Blessed One." On earlier occasions Jesus spoke of himself as God's "only begotten Son"; as such he calls God "my Father." This man standing in judgment obviously lays claim to a one-of-a-kind kinship with his heavenly Father — a co-naturality with God. This is the supposed blasphemy that occasions his death. (The priest-prosecutor points to the "smoking gun" which clinches his case.)

"Son of Man" only reinforces Jesus' avowal of his divinity. This is a very personal phrase found in the New Testament solely from the lips of Christ when speaking of himself. While it can sometimes mean something as simple as "man," in the context Jesus employs from Daniel the prophet it speaks of the glorified Judge at the Last Judgment, seated in honor with God and enwrapped in the splendor of Yahweh's presence. As such, Jesus' unique Sonship is canonized and glorified. The jury got the message. There is no need for further witnesses since the professed identity is evident. And so Jesus Ben Joseph goes to the cross — as Son of God. (The demons were right after all!)

What Man Has Ever Spoken as This Man?

Spending his last days in exile on St. Helena, the Emperor Napoleon's thoughts turned to religion. Speaking of Christ, he reasoned: "There is no God in heaven, if a mere man was able to conceive and execute successfully the gigantic design of making himself the object of supreme worship, by usurping the name of God. Jesus alone dared to do this." Christ did dare to demand supreme worship; he likewise dared to use Yahweh's name as his own. There is a God in heaven who approved and blessed his beloved Son's claim by word and miracle. Jesus dared precisely because he was not a mere man.

As befits his claim of divine Sonship, Jesus does many things proper only to God: he forgives sins; he claims to belong to the ages, "Before Abraham came to be, I am"; he does in fact control the wind and the sea; he says, "the Father and I are one" and "he who sees me also sees the Father." He uses Yahweh's name for himself, he accepts worship from his disciples, and he demands from them the ultimate faith we call religion.

Perhaps the boldest and most compelling claim of Jesus was his assertion that he has an everlasting life to give. Indeed, he is "the Way, the Truth, and the Life." "I am the resurrection and the life" (Jn 11:25). "My sheep hear my voice. I know them and they follow me. I give them eternal life, and they shall never perish" (Jn 10:27-28). No mere man in his right mind has ever spoken like this! In the words of C. S. Lewis, "Either this man was, and is, the Son of God, or else a madman or something worse."

St. John's Gospel has "Christ, the Word of divine life" as a veritable theme from the opening lines: "In the beginning was the Word; the Word was in God's presence, and the Word was God . . . . Whatever came to be in him found life, life for the light of men." The Jesus of John's Good News cannot even sit by a water well without talking about his gift of eternal life. "Whoever drinks the water I give him will never be thirsty; no, the water I give shall become a fountain within him, leaping up to provide eternal life" (Jn 4:14). A common vine and its branches remind him at his last meal, "I am the vine, you are the branches. He who lives in me and I in him will produce abundantly . . ." (Jn 15:5). John, in a concluding statement of this Gospel theme, explains that he writes "to help you believe that Jesus is the Messiah, the Son of God, so that through this faith you may have life in his name" (Jn 20:31). Even John's first Epistle reiterates this same theme that we can go through death and come out of it alive — alive with the life of God himself. John saw it all as an eyewitness, and as such he avows:

This is what we proclaim to you: what was from the beginning, what we have heard, what we have seen with our eyes, what we have looked upon and our hands have touched — we speak of the word of life. (This life became visible; we have seen and bear witness to it, and we proclaim to you the eternal life that was present to the Father and became visible to us.) What we have seen and heard we proclaim to you so that you may share life with us (1 John 1:1-3).

The letter even concludes with the affirmation that Jesus is "the true God and eternal life."

Yahweh is very much alive, and his Son is the very image of his Father.

Life at the End of the Tunnel

The simple truth of the Gospel story is that Jesus, the Son of God, has come to give us life and life to the full. As brothers and sisters of Christ (like branches on the vine) we can be "dead to sin and alive to God." We have faith that we can come out of death very much alive, and even more alive, because someone has already done so. Jesus died our death, and all we have to look forward to is life such as God enjoys.

Any story about life eternal that ends in the death of the hero on a cross isn't much of a life story. For instance, the trouble with

Jesus Christ Superstar is that it ends when the story was just getting good! *Superstar* leaves us with the corpse of Jesus to dispose of as we will. St. Paul bluntly states, "If Christ was not raised, your faith is worthless" (1 Cor 15:17). No question about it, only someone who can "lay down his life" and "take it up again" has everlasting life to give. The Jesus story is not the tale of someone who promises life and then dies before delivery. No, the Jesus story is an eyewitness account of both Good Friday *and* Easter Sunday. Easter is the capstone to everything Christ ever said about sharing his gift of life — a gift he has and is. The earliest creed of the young Christian community is a faith most succinctly stated — "Jesus died and is risen. Therefore he is Lord of all."

When the salesman for cemetery lots comes to the door of a Christian, he hears the answer, "Sorry, but I don't believe in death!" The menace of human death holds no terror for Jesus' followers; the menacing tomb, after all, is empty. Christ the Word of Life is risen. Alleluia!

Citizen of Two Worlds

If we ask "Who is Jesus Christ?" the age-old answer of the Christian community is "God, the Second Person of the Trinity." If we ask "What is Jesus Christ?" we pose a very different sort of question. This query probes his nature, what quality of being he is, rather than examining his person. Since Jesus is, as he said, a divine person, he can obviously do anything God can do, which is to say that he has a divine nature. And since Jesus is also "born of woman," he likewise has a genuine human nature — "He is like us in all things, but sin." Mary's Son tires and becomes thirsty, he laughs and weeps, he is vulnerable to pain and death. Jesus of Nazareth is truly both God and man. These two sets of abilities meet and are united in the single person we call Jesus.

As a full-fledged citizen of both worlds, Jesus literally *is* the perfect mediator between heaven and earth. In him God and man truly meet, are reconciled, and are at peace. Jesus is the peace bridge between opposite shores; any who cross this bridge make their peace with God. Christ, likewise divine and human, is the Father's finest Word eloquently cabled in a language we perfectly well understand — Jesus is the Father's supreme utterance.

Any person has some aura of mystery, unless he is perfectly comatose. We might expect, then, that there is a mystery about Jesus of Nazareth that defies our ability to "psyche him out." For example, does the infant Jesus have cosmic knowledge? How God and man touch and work together coherently in this divine person, only God knows. With Job we again admit, "I have dealt with great things that I do not understand; things too wonderful for me, which I cannot know" (Job 42:3). Jesus is the great thing God has wrought! While we cannot completely solve Jesus, at the same time we find him the most intriguing and wholesome individual we have ever met. He literally "has it all together." We may not fully comprehend the mechanics of the Incarnation (God's Son becoming our brother), yet we can proclaim that it works beautifully. Gerald Manley Hopkins phrased it well when he wrote that "There met in Jesus Christ all things that can make man lovely and lovable."

Speaking of Mary

Fittingly enough, in an effort to forge adequate language to answer questions about Jesus, early Church Councils (300-400 A.D.) spoke about Mary to make their statements the more emphatic. Again, it is a matter of family ties — "Whose son is he?" — for it is by relationship that we come to identity. G. K. Chesterton wisely remarked that Mary is the touchstone of orthodoxy. What you say about the mother, you say about the son. So, the proclaimed virginity of Mary is not so much a comment on celibacy (versus marriage) as it is an assertion that Jesus does not need a human father. He already has, and always had, God as his real Father. And Mary is "ever virgin" as witness to the eternal Father-Son tie between them. God might have arranged things otherwise, but he decreed a unique virgin birth as his clearest statement that "This is my beloved Son."

The amazing Marian title "Mother of God" was not so much an effort at making Mary more prominent as it was a declaration of her Son's identity. Like any normal human being, Jesus is one person. He is not a schizophrenic, but more a single, well-integrated personality than anyone we have ever met. Who, then, is this single individual? This person is none other than the Second Person of that God who is triune; he is the very person of God himself. "Mother" indicates a relationship with a person, not just a kinship tie with a human body or a set of human abilities. Mary is the Mother of the person Jesus. Since that person is the perfect, divine image of God his Father, Mary is truly the "Mother of God." August as this title is for Mary, it primarily points to Jesus as one person, namely, God's own Son.

A third title of Mary rounds out the task of God's integration into the human family: "Spouse of the Holy Spirit." The Nicean Creed asserts that "by the power of the Holy Spirit he was born of the Virgin Mary and became man." In the words of the angel to Mary, "The Holy Spirit will come upon you and the power of the Most High will overshadow you; hence, the holy offspring to be born will be called Son of God" (Lk 1:34-35). "Overshadow you" is better rendered "lay over you," alluding to the act of conception. It was the Spirit of Holiness who engendered God in the flesh. God does not need an agent; he literally *is* the power or Spirit of life. Thus, the Incarnation is a work of the total Trinity community.

All in all, God the Father sent the Son through the Holy Spirit. In a way, this answers the query, "What difference does the Trinity make in our life with God?" In actual fact, the Triune God is the cause, agency, and effect of the God-Man Jesus Christ, Son of God and Son of Mary — and our Brother!

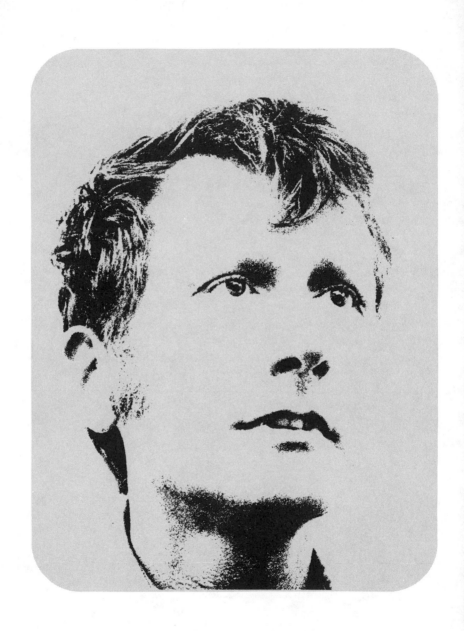

VI
Good News:
The Word of God

"Jesus Christ is and always has been what God has to say to mankind."* Is Jesus, then, God's game plan? Nothing less! More than simply a messenger, Christ is the Father's definitive message. In him we see the classic instance of the medium being the message. We might well have expected that anything definitive God has to say to us would be such a live wire and not a dead letter. Jesus comes not only to fulfill the Scriptures or to bear good news — he is the fulfilling Good News. He is the "fullness of God himself." "It is God the only Son, ever at the Father's side who has revealed him." In simple language Christ says, "I have come to show you the Father." In ideal terms, then, God's Son is not a message you learn, but rather a Word you personally experience. The apt question is not "Have you heard?" but "Have you met?"

If Jesus of Nazareth is the Father's first and last Word, what then is the content of the message? Surely Christ has some package of thought to give, some way of life to hand on. Indeed he has much to say, though much of it is not entirely original. Even the golden rule had already been preached by Rabbi Hillel a generation before the Messiah's coming: "Do not unto others what you would not have them do unto you." Jesus, however, has a way of summing up in his person all that had gone before. As Israel is God's chosen, so he is the Chosen One. As Israel is God's flock, so he is the Lamb of God. He speaks of himself as the sum of the Law and the Prophets, even the Temple of God on earth. So too, Jesus is also the synthesis of God's very ancient message. "Love one another" is, after all, a very old truth. Yet, in the Nazarene we see the ancient threads all drawn together and newly tied up.

Even the opening words of Christ's preaching career are borrowed. Like a soldier who snatches up a standard dropped by a fallen comrade, Jesus picks up and echoes the identical message of John the Baptizer. "From that time on [John's imprisonment] Jesus began to proclaim this theme: 'Reform your lives! The kingdom of heaven is at hand' " (Mt 4:17). So much of his preaching (as did John's) hinges on proclaiming the mysterious news of this "kingdom." It is strangely at hand, and yet to come. It

*The opening verse of St. John's Gospel from *Jesus,* Charles B. Templeton et al; Simon and Shuster, New York, N.Y., 1973. This is a fine contemporary paraphrase of the Gospels harmonized as one unified account.

is both weeds and wheat, a shining light on a stand and yet buried treasure. It is the pearl of great price which costs all and still the free gift of the Father to the poor in spirit. In this kingdom even life itself arises from dying to oneself! The paradox of the kingdom seems to be at the kernel of this mercurial message.

As was mentioned, Christianity is not so much belief in a static creed as it is the following of a person. Jesus is God's creed and ours. In a parallel sense, the kingdom of God is not so much a place we enter as it is a person who rules. The Christian faith is a personal allegiance, not the crossing of borders or the staking of a territorial claim. "The kingdom of God is within you." We have lost the Old English sense of the king's "dom" which emphasized the sovereign's power and jurisdiction rather than the realm over which he reigned. The better translations of the Bible now render "kingdom of God" as "the reign of God." The kingdom Jesus speaks of is more a state of mind than a state of boundaries; this inner kingdom eludes the map makers. Citizenship here is not a concern of residency or "owning a piece of the Rock" — you could not afford it! (And yet, of all commonwealths this is the easiest to become a citizen.) As in dancing, it is all a matter of who leads. The kingdom of God raises the question of who rules. So, it is not God's domain, but God's dominion which is at stake.

The Prayer of the Kingdom

It hardly comes as a surprise that the only formal prayer Jesus left us is kingdom-centered. In very Jewish fashion, Christ gives us a set of parallel petitions, three in all: "Thy name be hallowed, thy kingdom come, thy will be done." Exalting him, his name, or his will is the very coming of his kingdom — they are all the same thing in effect. If we let God take the lead, then the kingdom of heaven has truly come upon us.

The kingdom's coming is appropriately seen in the light of a rightfully restored monarchy. Monarchy is an archaic word. The age of kings is past, democracy is the wave of the present. "Do your own thing!" Obedience, too, seems obsolescent in an age of multiple emancipations. Giving way, much less giving sway, smacks of the medieval. Jesus, however, asks us to return to an age even more primeval. We are beckoned to return to the primal order of God's rule, a harmonious economy where God is Father and Jesus is Lord. This original order of God's affairs is restored by the proclamation of Jesus' lordship.

"Jesus is Lord!" is the oldest Christian creed to be found in the New Testament. It affirms that the Man of Nazareth is both Lord God and Sovereign-Lord. By recognizing and rejoicing in the Image of the Father in his Son, we acknowledge the Father himself and are accepted by him. "Whoever has seen me has seen the Father." To experience Jesus is to know and love the Father. Thus, every prayer of the kingdom customarily concludes "through Jesus Christ our Lord."

Difficulties fester when the would-be Christian would have Christ reign, but not rule. Often there is a lip-serving deference to Christian principles, but business as usual. We are all too familiar with the remaining figurehead kings who preside with no ruling power. Or again, one hears, "The kingdom of heaven on earth is too idealistic! We live in a real world; heaven and earth can never realistically meet, much less merge. The rule of the marketplace and the rule of Christ are totally incompatible." The basic premise of the Christian creed is that heaven and earth have indeed met and "kissed" (as the Psalms picture it) in the Lord Jesus. And this same amalgam of God's world and ours holds true for any who embody him. God's rule on earth is a radical idea, but only in the first dictionary sense of the word "radical" — the first and fundamental idea. Maybe a little primal therapy is the solution after all. Ah, but we are fearful of letting go so as to give another free reign; it is our besetting phobia. We want so to be masters of our own fate. Yet, the wonderful things of God cannot happen for us unless we do release our life, like the seed which gives way from its shell and seems to die in bearing much fruit.

Citizenship in the kingdom is not a difficult process; it is as easy as saying "thy kingdom come." As a result, life in the kingdom brings both hardship and joyful assurance, a challenge and a promise.

The Challenge

The story is told of W. C. Fields that while dying he asked a friend for a Bible. Surprised at this uncharacteristic request, the friend asked, "What would you want with a Bible?" Fields quipped, "Looking for loopholes." There are no loopholes or shortcuts to the Christian commitment. There is no cushy niche for the mediocre Christian. So much more than a Sabbath observance or a setting for a notable event, the kingdom is a consuming way of life. Remember, the kingdom is like a buried treasure or a priceless pearl for which a man sells all that he has. Yet, at any price it is still a bargain. There is a cost and Jesus would have us count the cost realistically, like the man in the parable who calculates beforehand to build his tower. There are crosses, but Jesus' "yoke is easy," his "burden light." His yoke, the sign of another's governance, rests so much easier than any of our own willful making.

Jesus is not asking anything which he has not first undertaken. He knew obedience. "Doing the will of him who sent me and bringing his work to completion is my food" (Jn 4:33). With marvelous insight St. Paul observes that "he learned obedience from what he suffered." He knew crosses. Any man who picked up John's banner would surely have a fate like John's awaiting him; Jesus needed no special insight during his public lifetime to know that the cross always hung over him. It was precisely because he was "obedient, even to the death" that Jesus the Christ is exalted as LORD (read Philippians 2:6-11). Yes, there are hardships and crosses, but the Lord Jesus is always in the lead along the pilgrim path beckoning us to follow.

The discipleship of Christ is nothing less than a response to the invitation, "If you love me, keep my word." And there has never been a challenge quite like Jesus' word:

Cherish fellow members of the kingdom. This is how all will know you for my disciples: your love for one another (Jn 13:35).

Treat anyone like Jesus himself. As often as you did it for one of my least brothers, you did it for me (Mt 25:40).

Do good for the unworthy, even your enemies. Do not set yourself against a man who wrongs you (Mt 5:44).

Be merciful and forgiving. If your brother . . . sins against you seven times a day, and seven times a day turns back to you saying, 'I am sorry,' forgive him (Lk 17:3-4).

Do not judge the merits of another. If you want to avoid judgment, stop passing judgment (Mt 7:1).

Share what you have. Let the man with two coats give to him who has none. The man who has food should do the same (Lk 3:11).

Cherish the poor. Parable of the Rich Man and the Poor Man (Lk 16:19-31).

Pray always. Pray always and never lose heart. Parable of the Judge and the Widow (Lk 18:1-8).

Be open to the invitations of God. Parable of the Great Banquet (Lk 14:16-24).

Risk all for the kingdom. Parable of the Talents (Mt 19:16-22). Parable of the Treasure and the Pearl (Mt 13:44-46).

The true pilgrim on the Christian way is still a shining wonder, because he follows a path which is absurdly out of step with those who follow their own paths. The life style of a Tom Dooley or a Mother Theresa of Calcutta cuts entirely across the make-it-and-flaunt-it secular syndrome. Still, we are somehow inexorably drawn by the sheer, beautiful daring of their "absurdity." When we see the word of the Gospel radically and literally practiced, we do instinctively recognize the "truth standing on its head."

God's kingdom is for the asking. True, we may enter his realm as suffering servants, but we soon enough reign with Christ as co-heirs of the kingdom. "Little ones, it has pleased your Father to give you a kingdom." The Christian birthmark, the Baptismal sign of entry, marks true sons and daughters of the Father, true brothers and sisters (adopted, though real) of the Son. Crossing into the kingdom confers royalty. Perhaps God's most extravagant wonderwork is his creation of a divine nobility out of earthy, peasant stock. Unlike the make-believe of Shakespeare's regal dramas, the Father makes us his own. The marvel is that God does not merely confer nobility — he truly creates it.

Count the cost, yes, but also count the promised blessings.

The Promise

When Abraham picks up Yahweh's challenge, he also lays hold of the promise that in him "all the communities of the earth shall find blessing." And just as we make vows in God's name, so Yahweh appropriately swears on and by himself. He can well do this because "God is true": it is his very nature to be faithful to his promises. This makes God's word a "sure thing," perhaps the only sure thing. In the course of time, the Jewish "people of the promise" found that Yahweh surely was faithful, as long as they hoped in the promise, and, like him, were true. What is more, we find that our blessings to come are not only assured, but greatly abundant. The promise is to the multitudes. The news of Jesus' renewed covenant speaks of the seed which becomes a veritable tree, of trees which bear "much fruit," of a harvest which is superabundant. "Good measure pressed down, shaken together, running over, will they pour into the fold of your garment" (Lk 6:38). In this sense the Christian lives the hope of the Gospel, not weakly wishing that God might remember his word, but assured that payment on the promise is already made out with our name on it. Not if, but when! Time is the only contingency before we come into full possession of the harvest.

Yet, how can we be so sure? Why, we even have security to cover payment of God's promissory note. Jesus is our security and assurance of promises kept. He is the Father's "yes" to all he has pledged. Christ, the Promised One, is our guarantor, the additional person who co-signs Yahweh's pledge. There is even a down payment on the great harvest, for we have our initial installment already in hand — the gift of the Spirit. This Spirit of Jesus is the foretaste and guarantee of the great harvest banquet. In this light, St. Paul writes of the stalwart courage by which we may brave difficulties. Christ is our security; the Holy Spirit is our first payment. We are very much like the Bostonian who saw no need to travel afar because he was already there!

In Jesus, the Father spells out his promise, and it is nothing short of fabulous. Like the apostles, we too instinctively ask what's in it for us: "Here we have put everything aside to follow you. What can we expect from it?" (Mt 19:27)

The prime gift is life. We shall be like God, alive forever. Entering into his life, we shall see God as he is. And as he is, so shall we be — in the mainstream of the Trinity. Enough said . . . there is no greater gift than this, that one give his life. With the gift of Jesus' Spirit, divine life is already ours. It happens then that no evil can defeat such a one, having "already passed from death to life."

The foretaste of the Spirit also includes blessings to be experienced even in this world:

When he comes . . . the Spirit of truth, he will guide you to all truth (Jn 16:13).

Your hearts will rejoice with a joy no one can take from you (Jn 16:22).

I solemnly assure you, there is no one who has left home or wife or brothers, parents or children for the sake of the kingdom of God who will not receive a plentiful return in this age . . . (Lk 18:29-30).

If you live in me, and my words stay part of you you may ask what you will — it will be done for you (Jn 15:7).

. . . they will manhandle and persecute you . . . bringing you to trial before kings and governors . . . I bid you resolve not to worry about your defense beforehand, for I will give you words and a wisdom which none of your adversaries can take exception to or contradict (Lk 21:12-15).

It was in one Spirit that all of us, whether Jew or Greek, slave or free, were baptized into one body (1 Cor 12:13).

Jesus shall gather into one all the dispersed children of God (Jn 11:52).

Signs like these will accompany those who have professed their faith: they will use my name to expel demons, they will speak entirely new languages . . . they will be able to drink deadly poison without harm, and the sick upon whom they lay their hands will recover (Mk 16:17-18).

The challenge and the promise of the kingdom is beautifully capsulized by King David in Psalm 16:
You, Lord, are all I have,
and you give me all I need;
my life is in your hands.

Abraham could hardly have dreamed how energetically and vividly God moves. He is on the move to us and for us and within us. God is very alive, so much so that in him we "live and move and have our being" — we live in his love.

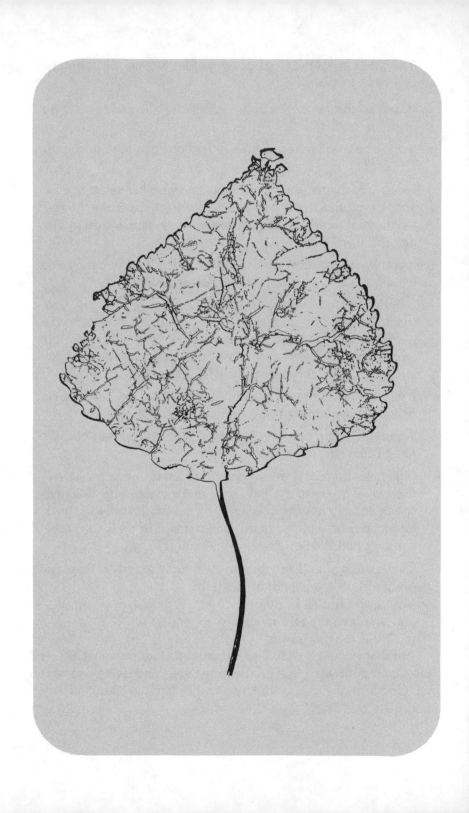

VII
Who Is
the Church?

Before the Vikings discovered and settled Iceland in the ninth century, a few Irish monks had already sought refuge on its solitary outer islands. Today, because of the vagaries of history, there are still fewer than a thousand Icelandic Catholics — only one half of one percent of the nation's population. When we consider that there is but a single Catholic Church structure, the Cathedral in Reykjavik, we might rightly guess that being an Icelandic Catholic is presently an urban experience. There is even the anxiety that living away from Reykjavik and its sole church means estrangement and possible alienation.

This concern for being "away from the Church" raises the deeper question "What is the Church?" Is the Church a building? Is it the hierarchy of clergy? Or is the Church God's assembled community, the bishop and his priests worshiping together with the people in the pews? The word "church" has varied meanings for different people. Listen in on any discussion of it and you will often hear as many definitions as there are persons speaking. Perhaps, though, we can peel away the layers of meaning and come to the essential "Church" by a process of elimination.

Church history tells us that houses for worship were a relatively late luxury of the Christian community. Only after Constantine's Edict of Milan (313 A.D.) could the Christians "come out of the catacombs" to construct buildings suited to their liturgical needs. Previously they prayed in synagogues, broke the Lord's bread in their own homes, or simply worshiped *alfresco* (as in Acts 16:13). Obviously, then, the Church predates the time when it could find sanctuary in structures hallowed for its own rituals. The Church, therefore, need not be a steepled building. It is a mistake to confuse the Church with the brick and mortar parish plant; the building may be "a church," but it is not "the Church."

What about the bishops, priests, and deacons? They are often enough spoken of as embodying the Church. We say, for example, "The Church changes the liturgy," or "The Church takes a stand against capital punishment." What we mean here is that the ordained clergy, or at least those clergy who hold decision-making positions have spoken. Yes, God's flock has shepherds (just as Jesus assumed the task of shepherding and in turn appointed pastors), but any such authentic leaders would be mighty lonely without their followers. A shepherd needs his flock as much as they need him. The Church-at-heart could not be the clergy alone. (Bishops and priests are still discouraged from celebrating a solitary Eucharist.) "All chiefs and no Indians" is not an episcopal motto, much less an apt description of the Church.

Then the Church must be the entire People of God, that is, the bishop and his clergy assembled *with* the laity for worship — shepherds and flock together. This view of the Church as Christian assembly, however, raises serious questions about those lonely Irish hermits, solitary on their Icelandic islands. Do we have to be actual social members of Christ's family to be Christians? Certainly members of the Christian community are called upon to be social (unlike Charlie Brown of the Peanuts cartoon who claims, "I love my neighbor — it's just people I can't stand!"). God does call us together as a people, a tribe of his own. We are not, however, necessarily called to stand inexorably linked arm-in-arm, physically grafted to one another. Yes, we are ordinarily expected to worship in community since we come to the Father in the totality of our being. We cannot be closet Catholics!

Still, aside from ordinary practice, there were Irish hermits isolated on Icelandic islands and there are modern islanders living in remote fishing villages having no Church building or assembly. Yet, they, for all their isolation, can be very much in the mainstream of the Church; a monk alone in his hermitage and a lone fisherman praying in his ketch might well be the Church's spiritual powerhouses. Both the parish community trying to sing somewhat together and the solitary monk or fisherman praying alone are equally the Church at worship. Jesus has forged a new togetherness that depends not on physical or social contact, nor on the proximity of time and place, but a togetherness that is not even sundered by the intervention of death.

It belittles God's Church to claim that it is a long-lived, multinational corporation with headquarters in Rome and multiple branch offices at convenient sites around the globe. Speaking of Jesus' flock in such impersonal business terms misses by a wide mark. Like Christ himself, his Church is not some*thing,* but some*one.* Jesus' Ascension, marking his physical departure and return to the Father, did not terminate his presence in our midst. He is yet with us, "always, until the end of the world," as he promised. Jesus now moves among us in a novel way, his presence and power no less real because they are not tangible. The Carpenter of Nazareth did leave his friends in the bodily sense, only to be bonded with them in a more unique intimacy.

It is not mere poetic wordplay when Jesus says, "I am the head, you are the members," or "I am the vine, you are the branches." This is a statement of an authentic living-together-in-him experience. St. Paul is not simply manipulating rhetoric when he writes that "It pleased God. . .to reconcile everything in his person, both on earth and in the heavens" (Col 1:20). God is assembling a people far more together than physical or social contact could ever cement, and Jesus is the matrix of that assembly. This God on the move is moving us together into himself in a bond such as mankind has never otherwise experienced. Quite *literally* "In Christ we live and move and have our being." St. Paul (in 1 Corinthians 3:23) says of the Church: "All these are yours . . . and you are Christ's and Christ is God's." Now that's togetherness! And that togetherness in Christ is "the Church."

A Giant Step for Mankind

Before leaving the room of the Last Supper that Thursday evening to walk quite deliberately to his death, Jesus raised a last prayer to his Father over his close friends:

That all may be one as you, Father, are in me, and I in you; I pray that they may be one in us . . . . I have given them the glory you gave me that they may be one, as we are one — I living in them, you living in me — that their unity may be complete (John 17:21-23).

This togetherness that Jesus prays for (a prayer surely answered) is nothing short of the organic cohesion that a single, living body enjoys — not just a side-by-side association, but a genuine living union. This is the togetherness nature itself yearns for when she joins cells into organs, and organs into living systems, and life systems into a cohesive body which, in a healthy sense, fosters and loves itself. But why should the divine scheme of things stop short with sundry human individuals that could only loosely be called — fingers crossed and tongue in cheek — the human family? (Even the most Utopian of societies would still remain an association of persons rather than a perfect communion.)

The priest-scientist Teilhard de Chardin mused that the process of evolution is not simply somewhere man has been, but also a greater someone mankind is becoming. Why, he asked, should not human individuals be incorporated into a yet more vast living body? Why are they not embodied into a yet more elite life system? And what, or rather who would that be? Jesus of Nazareth is that vastly greater someone who encompasses and enlivens all who come, not just unto, but into him. While a theologian could talk of our adoption by God, a horticulturist would more likely speak of God's grafting us to Christ, the vine stock. (In the agricultural phrases of John's Gospel, the Father is the "vinegrower.") Since evolution (God's gardening) is ongoing, why could not a special human being, as a kind of new Adam, take that "one giant step for mankind," that giant stride that makes the family of man a single living organism — one body? The Lord Jesus prays to his God-Father for nothing short of this absolute embodiment of the human race into himself: "That they may be one, as we are one . . . . I living in them, you living in me — that their unity may be complete." When "God gives the growth" he really gives the growth! Jesus guaranteed his followers, shortly before his arrest:

Anyone who loves me will be true to my word, and my Father will love him; we will come to him and make our dwelling place with him . . . . (John 14:23).

So many Christians have yet to grasp what it means to be "in Christ." They assume it resembles membership in the Rotarians or the Jaycees, only more spiritual. But "Church" is not a matter of belonging to the roster of a heavenly club that gives access to a celestial clubhouse. When St. Paul says that the Christian is a "member of Christ" he means something much more thoroughgoing than a membership roster or a group association. Paul depicts an ongoing creation by which God literally grafts us to himself so that, in actuality, "he lives now, not I."

This working out of a godly evolution is still in process. The Father is yet absorbing through and into Jesus all who respond to him in love. This actual, organic union in Christ is "the Church." The Epistle to the Ephesians says it so eloquently:

God has given us the wisdom to understand fully the mystery, the plan he was pleased to decree in Christ, to be carried out in the fullness of time: namely, to bring all things in the heavens and on earth into one under Christ's headship (Ephesians 1:9-10).

Therefore, Paul insists, we are "a dwelling place for God in the Spirit."

Spin-offs

The program launching men into space has fortunately generated sideline benefits, such as transistors and electronic miniaturization. The heart pacemaker, for instance, is partially a space program spin-off. An authentic understanding of the Church as God's people literally embodied in Christ would likewise have profound side benefits. The conclusion of the Apostles Creed

I believe in the Holy Spirit,
the Holy Catholic Church,
the Communion of Saints,
the forgiveness of sins
the resurrection of the body,
and the life of the world to come

is a veritable litany of such byproducts. Lenin once claimed that an idea is the most powerful force in the world. Once the idea of Church as Christians alive in Jesus takes hold, it generates a wide outer grid of energetic truths.

So many today think quite poorly of themselves; they do not love themselves. In Christ, everyone, no matter what his or her drawbacks, is the only child of a divine Father; each living member of this Christ-Church is that beloved Someone in whom the Father is "well pleased." What a difference it would make if we fully appreciated that we are the limbs by which Jesus presently imposes hands and blesses this world — that the Lord Jesus, this moment, ordinarily touches and heals this troubled globe only through us! Realizing that we are cast in a stellar role, we would come to a richer sense of our own personal worth. So we should think well of ourselves: we have more than VIP connections, for we are royally "born of God."

If God ordinarily realizes his concern for humankind through us, then the possibility opens that this or that person, because of us, may not come to know God as loving, or only imperfectly so. Many experience the Father defectively because they have never known the selfless love of a parent. Their very image of "father" is flawed by memories of a defective human father or mother. (God surely has the best features of both parents.) If we presently embody Jesus, the Father's image, then even God is usually limited to the likeness we project. "Pillars of the Church," those uprights of the Temple which is Christ, either uphold Jesus as the true image of the Father, or keep getting in the way. Pillars either obstruct one's view or lead the line of sight directly to a focus on God.

Sharing the body and life pulse of Christ also puts us in instant communication with every other limb of his body, be he Irish monk of a past age, a modern martyr imprisoned, or someone dear an ocean away. The dream of modern communication is instantaneous dialogue with anyone, anywhere. If the scientists checked the records, they would find that Christ already has the patent on it. After all, Christians are living the identical life of Jesus in whom there are no barriers of time or place, or even death. This communion of saints, to use the time-honored phrase, usually calls to mind a poetic fellowship, rather than the organic bond that enables one Christian to live the same Christ-life of another, that empowers all Christians to be animated by the one soul of God.

We are often rather oblivious of this instant communication resource, since we do not see the wires or cannot measure the radio waves. Although the lines of connection are often unseen, yet the welfare of one affects all; the integrity of all affects the least individual. We are so much more whole and holy because of a single monk praying on an uncharted island. Paul teaches that "If one member suffers, all the members suffer with it; if one member is honored, all the members share its joy '(1 Cor 12:26). It sometimes happens that Christian missionaries working in North Africa or the Orient do not personally see the fruits of their labors. The Bible tells us as much: "One sows, another reaps" (Jn 4:37), but it is God who gives the growth. This mysterious growth may even be in another place, in another era — the life of the Spirit is like that, "blowing where he will." All this guarantees, however, that the works of Christ we do are never unfruitful.

How reassuring that we can call upon the litany of saints as colleagues and co-workers. They can make up what we somehow lack. In Christ, no member need ever feel inadequate or be lonely. No one need ever feel at a distance from the "absolute saints." Perhaps we have never considered the calendared saints as our intimates, but that is the case. "You are strangers and aliens no longer . . . you are fellow citizens of the saints and members of the household of God." Furthermore, the organic bond of this union relates Mary to us in a sense beyond mere poetic fancy. If Mary is the Mother of Jesus in the flesh, we are now that flesh and she is our mother.

Being Jesus personified brings with it one of the magnificent gifts of the Spirit; we can always call God "Father," just as Jesus did. Our identity with Christ is such that, whenever we raise our voices to him, our Father hears the call of his beloved Son Jesus. Along with brother Christ, we too can boast that "the Father always hears my voice." And why shouldn't he? — after all, we are part of the family. Going even beyond the polite address of traditional prayers, we can pray "Papa-God, this is Jesus. . . ." That, after all, is how the Lord prayed and how our Father knows us. The early Church remembered very few of Jesus' native Aramaic words, but "Abba" (literally "Daddy") was one of them. This is precisely how the first Christians prayed in imitation of their Lord. "Abba" means that the king of the universe is our true Father. That makes us pretty well connected. We are royalty at the very least!

Perhaps, best of all, St. Paul reassures us that "in Christ there is no condemnation." Real or false guilt, then, need not be the crippler it is for so many, so long as we are "in Christ." After all, Jesus of Nazareth is the sinless one. By a kind of osmosis, let us say, his holiness confers forgiveness and healing, wholeness and integrity. Jesus, our elder brother, stands ahead of us before the Father. The Father looks and sees only his well-favored Son. It is not our worth that allows us to stand upright before our Creator — such standing is neither earned nor deserved. We are simply designated by what the British would call "royal grace and favor." It is Jesus who has done our earning and deserving; it is he who bridges our holiness gap, the pitfalls of which the saints are well aware. (Strangely enough it is the "absolute saints" who are most keenly aware of their unworthiness.)

Back to the Womb

Just how does one become a member of this larger body, the cosmic Christ? From the very onset Jesus makes it clear that the grafting process is only by gift of invitation: "No one comes to me unless the Father draw him." In his own characteristic, mysterious way, God beckons and draws. Christians have too often thought of themselves as *"the* chosen" rather than simply "chosen"; God's choosing by no means implies that we are choice. Remember that often enough he selects the unlikely — which choice is a hallmark of his. It is ofttimes the most needy and destitute who appreciate their need for God; they have the kind of handle he can grasp.

Every member of Christ has his or her own spiritual odyssey to tell. Meetings with God are much like the mysterious intersecting of a man and a woman who eventually become husband and wife. At times it seems like the happenstance of the right person knocking on the wrong door. Such was the case with Bishop Fulton Sheen who accidently met the violinist Fritz Kreisler and his wife while seeking the apartment of a friend who lived on the same floor. That knock was for them an encounter with grace, an invitation to which the Kreislers responded. Luck had nothing to do with it. Few, though, are struck down in blinding light like Saul of Tarsus. More often than not it is the compelling witness of a person who already enjoys that flow of God's life and love, like "living waters within them bubbling up unto everlasting life." Those who have it cannot help but flaunt it. Their personal silent sermons are the shortest and the most eloquent. These individuals are the hand of God knocking at the door — which is what the Church is all about. Still, they are only the occasion. Grafting into the person of Christ is yet a more intimate and subtle meeting that wells from a free response to God's love.

In order to embody ourselves in Jesus in a truly authentic way, something more telling and thorough than a gesture of initiation (say a knighthood tap on the shoulder) has to happen. Gestures or exotic ritual do not remake the man. God must re-create us if we are to enjoy "life from above." The designation "born-again Christian" is right on the mark. The Pharisee Nicodemus, when meeting with Jesus, is not very perceptive; yet, he does ask the right question: "How can a man be born again?" We cannot draw upon new life power unless we have a new power generator. There can be no different life without a fresh life source — a new soul.

We are born with a human soul that empowers us to live and move on the human scene. God the Creator must then invest us with a new soul or spirit if we are to operate at his apex of life. In fact, he will have to reconceive and animate us with his own soul! "... No one can enter into God's kingdom without being begotten of water and Spirit" (Jn 3:5). Nothing short of rebirth with God's own Spirit-power will suffice. ("Soul" is a Greek concept; Jews would speak of "heart" instead.) The prophet Ezekiel describes just such a heart transplant. The rebirth that grafts us into the person of Jesus so that we literally "live in God" is the implant of Jesus' power source, his soul, which is the crux of his love-life with the Father. Whoever lives by this Spirit is as authentically Jesus as if he had been cloned. Such "birth from above" gives us soul-power so that we have "that mind which is in Christ." And our energy is such that, as the Lord promised, "the works I do you also shall do."

In human experience each of us has his own individual soul. Now, in Christ, all Christians share a novel experience — we have one and the same Spirit! The one Spirit of Jesus and his Father enlivens each and all. In the earthly realm, there is nothing quite comparable. This means, then, that "you are not your own." No member of Jesus lives in splendid isolation, going his own willful way as a kind of cancer. "You are the one Christ," Paul is at pains to explain. (Paul would probably vote Church disunity the worst of evils.) All members foster one another as we would expect of a healthy body. In effect, the Church is God loving himself wholesomely and creatively.

The mutual care one member of the Christ-Church should have for building up all the others gives rise to the apt label "the Servant Church." "He is greatest who is the servant of the rest." If God's people are to be Jesus here and now, they necessarily represent the Son of Man who has "come to serve." (Washed any feet lately?)

Granted, St. Paul has a way with words. In his letter to the Ephesians he captures that unique, never-before-encountered experience called "the Church":

You form a building which rises on the foundation of the apostles and prophets, with Christ Jesus himself as the capstone. Through him the whole structure is fitted together and takes shape as a holy temple in the Lord; in him you are being built into this temple, to become a dwelling place for God in the Spirit (Eph 2:20-22).

Joan of Arc never had St. Paul's eloquence, but in her own simple manner she reached to the essence of "Church." Answering the judges at her trial, Joan said, "I see no difference between Jesus Christ and the Church. They are all the same to me!" It seems, then, that God is on the move, and in us.

VIII
Signs Used
by Jesus

St. John's Gospel shows his uneasy apprehension about later generations of Christians who would not have the same physical encounter with Jesus he himself treasured. John's First Epistle recalls his cherished intimacy with the Lord, whom "we have heard . . . have seen with our own eyes . . . looked upon and our hands have touched." But what of future Christians who could not hear and touch the Lord? In response John makes much of the apostle Thomas who had similar difficulties about believing without seeing. We even hear a new beatitude for subsequent Thomases: "Blest are they who have not seen and have believed." This would hopefully bolster those who could not be there to witness the Lord's "signs," as John calls them. John is writing for future generations who might well say, "Not seeing and yet believing may be blest, but it still seems quite a disadvantage!"

John, however, is also wise enough to know that Jesus did not ascend to the Father to achieve a neat exit, but rather to move and act in the world in another way. The Church community was not at all orphaned; it was to be Christ still present and palpable, to experience his Power (as the Spirit is called), to continue working his "signs." Later ages of Christians are not cheated by being at a distance in time from Christ. Just as Jesus is God made physical, so the Church is Christ Incarnate still working in a very visible way.

What has Christ done for us lately? He is, as he promised, accomplishing the same works — and even greater — that John saw. God's Son has the advantage of not being limited by time lines; and he can consequently stretch through time his worship of the Father, his forgiving words, his laying on of healing hands, his breaking bread at table. Being timeless, Jesus now performs his signs in his new body, the community of the Church. If we think that the liturgy of the Church is just so much chant and incense, then we have misread the signs of the times. Unhampered by temporal limits, the same person of Jesus moves and speaks with the same power, but in a new age.

The Mass and the sacraments are as much a tangible meeting with the Lord as the encounter Zacchaeus had with him. If we have trouble remembering Zacchaeus, an early New England primer depicts him vividly: "Zacchaeus, he/Did climb a tree/Our Lord to see." This chief tax collector of Jericho was also trying to "see what Jesus was like." Being rather short of stature, he climbed a sycamore tree to observe him. The Lord looked up and said to Zacchaeus, as he still does to any Christian in the Mass and the sacraments, "I mean to come to your house today." (We do not have to be up a tree to meet Jesus now, but it often helps.)

Christ's style of acting is altered at present, but he is yet moving in the direction of anyone who has eyes to see and ears to hear, whatever his stature. Karl Adam writes that "the sacraments are nought else than a visible guarantee . . . that Jesus is working in the midst of us." Many of Jesus' contemporaries did not even then see and hear him for what he was; others are even now oblivious to the liturgical signs that "Jesus of Nazareth is passing by." Ideally, the liturgy should be a celebration of the fact that we have, in our own fashion, seen and touched the Lord.

Down to Earth

The German poet Goethe calls the sacraments "sensuous" signs. I think he means that they are highly keyed to the senses. As a real man in a material world, the Carpenter of Nazareth is completely rooted in the concrete. Even the language of his Hebrew culture is quite limited to sensory images and material allusions. To speak his message Jesus is forced to tell stories and weave metaphors. To this physical world he brings Spirit and truth, but only by using tangibles to project the true Spirit. Jesus is not simply a preacher on a pillar spouting abstract maxims. No, he does the works of his Father by touching the leprous, literally raising up the paralyzed, hugging the children, breaking bread and sharing wine. We feel the kinetic energy of his touch. The risen Lord is a man, not a ghost, as he tells his amazed followers that Easter evening. Christ continues to be tangible in the Church by using water, bread, wine and oil, the laying on of hands, a couple's word of commitment, a sinner's confession of guilt as material signs of his activity.

The Gospels complain of those who have lost the ability to interpret the signs of the times. This type of illiteracy is nicely illustrated in the story of a racing fan at a horse race who watched the betting habits of a priest who was trying his hand at the sport. He noticed that every time the priest blessed a certain horse at the paddock, that horse would win. Finally, sure that he had a winning system, the gentleman noted the horse picked for the ritual and bet all his money on that blessed number. But the horse lost! Finding the priest afterward, the man complained of his losses. The priest responded, "Your trouble is, you don't know the difference between a simple blessing and the Last Rites of the Church." Perhaps that is our problem too. We seem to have lost our sense for reading the liturgical signs aright.

What Jesus did for his fellow citizens was not empty ritual or awesome gestures calculated to amaze. The signs of his ministry actually healed the paralytic and actually returned a once-dead son to his greiving mother. There was too much mere ritual in his own time for Jesus to add any additional sleight of hand. The point is, the Lord's signs (words and gestures) work. What they indicate, they give. They speak of renewed life and health and they actually give it. If, for example, a STOP sign were somehow sacramental, it would really accomplish what it demonstrates and stop our cars. The Mass and the sacraments do what they show and tell.

Often enough, too, Jesus' physical healing was an indication of an inner healing of heart. That paralytic went home heavier for the mat he carried, but lighter for the burden of guilt lifted from his shoulders. Such Biblical events effectively using sensuous signs to touch body and soul are, as the Church teaches, "a living and continuous reality through all the ages." Any such authentic meeting with one's God is, of course, a mutual encounter entered into freely from both sides. There is no magical push-pull-click-click effect, for it depends on what those involved bring to it. These liturgical signs work, but only if we come to them in faith. Remember that at times even the Lord himself "could work no miracles there . . . so much did their lack of faith distress him." So any sacramental encounter will be as fruitful as we perceive and expect it to be. (Even Christ has little room to be creative in an efficiency apartment.)

Sign Language

We often misread the signs of meeting with our God, not only because we are at a distance in time, but because we are likewise removed from Jesus' own culture which readily discerned the meaning of simple gestures and natural elements. In an arid climate where water sources are very limited, water literally means life. Adding fresh liquid to barren, rocky soil brings the desert into blossom. Water in a wasteland is a precious, if not sacred, commodity, tipping the scale between life and death, between fruitfulness or desiccation.

Our simple pouring of Baptismal water does not amply demonstrate to us the death by drowning in the waters and rising to renewed life that Baptism by immersion graphically shows. We get the sense of cleansing, but not quite an awareness of entering into the death, burial, and Resurrection of the Lord.

We have likewise lost the sign-sense of oil, previously a cure-all liniment. Notice that the Good Samaritan of the parable administers oil as first aid. Oil was also a rich, aromatic ointment poured on honored guests. Christ himself once remarked that his host neglected to anoint him, while the sinful woman did. On occasion, oil was the hallmark of royal and priestly acclaim.

And does the laying on of hands speak to us significantly? It was a natural gesture so easily understood by the Old Testament mentality. An imposition of hands imparted Jacob's blessing and Moses' choice of his successor Joshua; and the same was done for the ordination of Levites and the installation of rabbis in Christ's own time. According to the Jewish mind, the hand was the person's power to bless, choose, and heal. So when Jesus blessed the children, he, like any rabbi, "embraced them and blessed them, placing his hands on them." When ministering to the sick, Jesus "laid hands on each of them and cured them." The onlookers expectedly praised Jesus' hand power which they saw exercised. It is not surprising then that we find the early Church laying on hands, as the Lord did, to choose, to empower, to heal.

Unfortunately, the sense of Biblical signs is more or less lost on what one critic has called "a generation of scriptural illiterates." It is true that the signs of the liturgy speak of God's ever-present power, but we sometimes read them as a dumb show of bygone events. We should not be surprised, then, that the Church has redesigned the liturgy from time to time and even designated new and more significant words and gestures as the essential rite of some sacraments. Pope John was not the first in the Church to think of "aggiornamento"; updating its sign language to "today" has been a perennial concern.

What God has ever said by sign language — be it a burning bush, a Passover meal, an uplifted cross, an empty tomb — is never void or meaningless. The Hebrew Scriptures emphasize that the Word of God, however it is communicated, is never impotent. So also, God speaks powerfully in the Eucharist and in other sacramental signs. His designs are never speculative blueprints, but working models.

Remembrance of Things Present

The ghost of Hamlet's father in the Shakespeare play is forced by the onset of dawn to capsulize his message in an insistent "Remember me!" Obviously he means something more conclusive than just a lingering memory of his cruel murder. And Hamlet understands it in more than just the passive sense; he gets the message that what is required is not a memorial service, but appropriate action in the present.

It is in much the same sense that the Jews yearly enter into the Paschal meal at Passover. A Passover supper is so much more than a food commemoration of what God did for his people in centuries past; it is a celebration of what he is presently accomplishing on their behalf. Modern-day Jews still apply the Passover text to themselves in saying, "We were once slaves of Pharaoh in Egypt, but the Lord brought us out of Egypt with his strong hand. . . ." Passover continues and re-presents that liberation experience. Unlike a slide show of a past voyage, it enacts God's passage in their midst at this moment.

As an observant Jew, Jesus at his last Passover Supper speaks an insistent "Remember me!" in the very same sense — not to reflect a memory, but to relive a liberation. In today's Mass any Christian can rightly say, "I was a slave to evil, but the Lord brought me out of bondage with his strong hand." Our present passage from death to life is no less real.

In handing bread and wine to his friends, Jesus surely identified himself with these life elements. But why did he use both samples of food? Surely bread alone would have been sufficient for Jesus to convey, "I am the bread of life" and "I am always with you." To the Jewish mind the total man is flesh animated by blood (rather than our Greek notion of body enlivened by soul). In bread and wine, his flesh and blood, we meet the complete, living person of Jesus. "The man who feeds on my flesh and drinks my blood remains in me, and I in him" (Jn 6:55). In effect he is saying, "Here I am, flesh and blood."

The Lord, however, is alive and present in a particular manner, by way of that greatest love — "laying down one's life for his friends." He shows his "body broken" and his "blood shed." To the Jewish mind death meant bloodshed, the separation of the life-blood from the body. In fact, by Hebrew reckoning the Last Supper after sundown was celebrated on the same day as his death; for Christ there was little distinction between what he did at table on Mount Zion and what he did on the cross of Mount Calvary. It was the same bloodletting and death with only a change of style. This particular aspect of the Last Supper St. Paul is at pains to impress on the Corinth community: "Every time, then, you eat this bread and drink this cup, you proclaim the death of the Lord until he comes!" (1 Cor 11:26)

Unlike the apostles there in the Upper Room, we have the advantage of Monday morning hindsight, for we further remember that the darkness of Friday was followed by the brightness of Easter Sunday. No bread box of a tomb could hold the Bread of life. In the Mass we have ever after experienced the Lord Jesus as he now lives, alive and whole. (A ritual joining of a particle of bread to the wine, uniting flesh and blood, reminds us that death was only a passing episode in the life of Christ.) So the Lord's Supper remembers and relives the entire Paschal event, the death and Resurrection of the Lord. To share this meal is to take a tour through and out into the light at the end of the tomb.

Breaking bread with the risen Lord always involves the intimacy of sharing his death and life odyssey — so shared, in fact, that we can live his life as equally as he can die our death. The altar is both table and tomb, supper and sacrifice. The long history of the liturgy in various eras has emphasized either the sacrificial death or the life-giving meal. In reality, Jesus' death-to-life is a total package tour, the ultimate Crucifixion-Resurrection trip still open and available in the Mass. The itinerary of this passage is really quite simple — if we enter into Christ's death, he catches us up into his life. (Now that's the choice way to travel, port going out and starboard coming home.)

The events that the Lord's Supper relives move fluidly through time and beyond it. The table-tomb puts us in touch with a past historical event that we can tap into at our own leisure time. This is also an event with a future, for "we proclaim the death of the Lord until he comes." The first three Gospels all look to a fulfillment of the kingdom as they recount the words of the Eucharist. "I tell you, I will not drink this fruit of the vine from now until the day when I drink it new with you in my Father's reign" (Mt 26:29). The Eucharist marks time until that moment when the physical presence of the Lord, once again before us, makes the ritual presence obsolete. The Jews traditionally conclude the Passover meal with the acclamation, "Next year in Jerusalem!" Perhaps the Mass should end with the similar response, "Next year in the heavenly kingdom!"

IX
Christ-Touches:
The Seven Sacraments

The Israelites, by God's power, had escaped servitude in Egypt by coming through the waters of the Exodus. Yet they had not only come *from* something they had also come into the desert *for* something. At Sinai the people of Israel heard just how astonishing that something was:

> If you hearken to my voice and keep my covenant, you shall be my special possession, dearer to me than all other people, though all the earth is mine. You shall be to me a kingdom of priests, a holy nation (Exodus 19:5-6).

Their "baptism" through the waters was a deliverance for dedication; the God of their Fathers wished to consecrate them as his "special possession" — his treasure. This involves a unique relationship called a blood covenant. Implied too is a commitment to a special mission and a way of life.

It happens in many cultures that two persons, not otherwise related, mingle their blood together as a sign of new kinship (for example, the woodsman and the American Indian becoming blood brothers). This makes the two "family" so to speak, for they now have a blood tie. The Lord of the universe offered such a bond, beyond even that of intimate friendship. He wanted Israel to become "family." In Biblical language, Yahweh does speak of his family ties to "his people" — now he is Father, again he is husband, but always one of the family.

Any such Bible covenant for kinship, be it in the time of Abraham or Moses, David or Christ, is always initiated by God's choosing, freely answered by his chosen, and solemnized by some sort of blood ritual. Ever after it is remembered and renewed by a memorial sign. Circumcision was such a sign for Abraham; the observance of the Sabbath was Moses' souvenir of the covenant. Usually it was a sign that distinctly marked or distinguished one, even physically, as consecrated and committed. Our rites of Christian Initiation (Baptism, Confirmation, and Eucharist) are such eloquent and effective signs of our own escape through the waters. Through them we arrive at a unique relationship: we become God's "special possession." We too are signed and sealed as his own people, a relationship which is ever after remembered and relived in the Eucharistic blood of the New Covenant.

It clarifies matters to think of Baptism, Confirmation, and the Eucharist as a package. The Church community, initially Jewish in the main, thought in terms of the three-fold entry of a convert (proselyte) into the family of Israel. Since neither the Jewish convert nor his forebears had passed through the Exodus experience, he would necessarily undergo a ritual bath; then, marked by circumcision, he would finally participate in the Passover meal. Every year thereafter he would signify his personal Exodus and covenant dedication in this solemn meal.

In the early Christian practice described in the Acts of the Apostles, a new follower of Jesus was, in quick succession, passed through the waters of Baptism, marked in Christ's image by the gift of the Spirit, and brought to the table to celebrate, "until he comes," the death-to-life passage of the risen Lord. Baptism, Confirmation, and Eucharist as a single rite of initiation is still the custom of Eastern Rite Christians and has recently been restored in the West as the three-step entrance of adult converts. All this bonds the new disciple in a blood relationship to God himself. The new-born Christian, though, is something much more than a "special possession" of the Almighty — now, having been "born from on high," he is possessed by God.

Mission Possible

The mark of Christ goes so much deeper than the ritual cross signed upon the forehead of the baptized or confirmed. We might call Baptism and its completion in Confirmation the sacraments of conformation; for they not only mark us but literally conform us to the likeness of Jesus in thought and deed. St. Paul thinks of this insignia of the covenant in terms of a stamp that marks a debt as "paid" or a brand that perpetually marks a Roman soldier for service. Paul is even more to the point when he talks of the Christian as "sealed" by the Holy Spirit. The Spirit of God, like a signet ring in wax, impresses and molds us to an authentic image of the Savior.

We do not lose our own identity; yet, our consciousness is raised, our judgments and instincts so heightened that it is the Lord Jesus thinking and acting. This condition has been described as follows: "It is the Spirit who makes us Christlike, who shapes the very roots of our capacity to think and love like Christ." We are, however, not simply acting out a Christian role model; the "new person" reborn by water and the Spirit is Christ on the move. In the new order, the seal of Christ's image given in Baptism actually reshapes the disciple, as the signet ring does the wax.

What is the purpose of this reshaping? We should not be surprised that we are being marked and molded for a mission. Our mission, should we accept it, is to be a holy and priestly people — holy because in obedience we shall love as Jesus did, priestly because in so loving we too will give our life as an offering for many. If, however, we fail in this mission, we will self-destruct.

This is the identical mission that so many of the Israelites failed once they had journeyed on from Sinai. They somehow reasoned that they could enjoy both the manna from heaven as well as the fleshpots of Egypt. And in a half-hearted attempt to follow the Pillar of Fire across the desert while still retreating to an Egyptian life style, they self-destructed. The truly impossible mission is attempting to counterfeit a fuzzy image of Jesus while at the same time trying to make the scene elsewhere. But ours is a jealous God, covetous of his special family possession. Being holy as our God is holy means living out wholly the total commitment that an exchange of blood promises. And this may mean shedding a little of life's blood along the way.

The sign of Confirmation appears, over the centuries, to have become a Christian Bar Mitzvah; as a kind of latter-day Crusader, a maturing youngster took his oath to become a "soldier of Christ." (We would expect vows made on the hilt of a sword rather than an anointing with oil on the forehead.) If Confirmation is received long after Baptism, it is most certainly an opportunity to affirm personally what was promised by godparents on our behalf. Still, the crux here is not so much what we can do for God, but what God will do for us.

The fantasy novels of Ursula Le Quin entitled *The Earthsea Trilogy* make the distinction between "the life of being" and "the life of doing." The Anointing with the Holy Spirit takes the new-born state of Baptism and galvanizes it with *life power*. It realizes in high relief that Christ image and actualizes it in motion as "the life of doing" the will of the Father. To better understand this, note the difference between still photography and 3-D color motion pictures. The special gift of the Spirit, already received in Baptism, then releases the potential print given at spiritual birth and fully projects it. The "gift" given at every Christian's personal Pentecost is the same Spirit of life and love exchanged between the divine Father and Son. God gives as gift his own medium of exchange who, beyond holy, is Holiness himself. Who could better chip away at us to sculpt the living profile of Jesus than his own Spirit! He alone knows the answer to the question, "What is the Son of God really like?" Jesus was, after all, the veritable image of the Father "conceived by the Holy Spirit."

When God gives a gift, he does not stint — he offers not just any gift, but *the* Gift. On the topic of the Father's utter largesse, Jesus teaches, "If you, with all your sins, know how to give your children good things, how much more will the heavenly Father give the Holy Spirit to those who ask him" (Lk 11:13). It is, moreover, the Gift that keeps giving — according to the capacity of the receiver. As one of the enduring sacraments, Confirmation is the sacrament to grow on. Any power is restless; the creative power of God is eminently so. The Spirit is in perpetual motion, constantly shaping to the full stature of Christ whatever is maleable and soft-hearted. Jesus' boast "I am with you all days" is made good by the Spirit power of Baptism; Jesus' insistence "that you bear fruit" is made good by the Spirit power of Confirmation. Even the cynical Erasmus recognized that the Spirit called Holy is necessarily productive when he comments, "Nor shall I believe that you are in the Spirit except I behold in you the works of the Spirit." Anyone confirmed is signed and sealed for a mission and the sign should read "Spirit at Work."

Working Models

Two sacraments specifically supply and send the Christian out on mission. Both delineate a profile of Jesus that is distinctly priestly; both fulfill the commission of the Old and New Covenants to be "a kingdom of priests, a holy nation." Ordination, for one, readily comes to mind as a priestly assignment. I wonder, however, if we ever think of marriage as a call to priesthood.

The sign of Matrimony is a marvelous instance of lay involvement in the "kingdom of priests." The partners truly minister the sacrament to one another, so much so that in exceptional cases the priest-witness can be dispensed with. Any such covenant commitment to share fully with another God's life-giving love would have to be both a ministry and a sacrament. Only the lovers and life-givers themselves could minister that kind of full exchange. And, like ordained priesthood, it is one of the permanent, ongoing signs, shaping the persons to their loving role over a lifetime. When a couple talks of having received the sacrament of Matrimony on a certain date so many years ago, it sounds very much like a bygone event, rather than a viable and current exchange of holiness. That kind of involvement in God's love could not be a "sometime thing," as the romantic ballad tells it. Husband and wife, for every moment of their life together, administer to one another. They are always the medium of exchange for God's love — and that passes for a fine, working definition of priesthood.

Marriage partners are often the most vivid signs of love's endurance, love's fidelity, love's occasional ecstasy. But more than a reasonable facsimile of these, they actually sweep each other up into God's love life, which is perfectly enduring, faithful, and ecstatic. They do not love like God. They are God himself loving! Their centerness in each other is so much God's that their mutual love is personalized in the living soul of a child. The Trinitarian aspect is evident since the love between them is not merely something, but a spirited someone. Affectionate couples do not, as they might imagine, invent love. "God is love," and any pair genuinely caring for one another must enter into his love. The game of love is always played in God's ball park.

A marriage partner becomes a specialist, dedicating him/ herself to a special someone. In the Letter to the Ephesians partners are asked to love each other as they would themselves. "Husbands should love their wives as they do their own bodies." As if that were not sufficient, they are also called, even empowered, to devote themselves to their special partners with the measure that Christ has loved them. "Husbands, love your wives, as Christ loved the Church." (And that goes for wives as well!) In Ephesians we see Yahweh's gift of himself in marriage to Israel and Jesus the bridegroom's espousal to his people now realized in a working model — sacramental marriage. Karl Adam notes, "The fact that Christ and his Church are one sole body is realized anew in every Christian marriage." Any such working model should show in miniature how its exemplar moves. Just so, married couples live out a witness to God's love that is necessarily enduring, faithful, unconditional, and creative. Marriage cannot be renewable after a time, open to other lovers, rife with conditional escape hatches, or always shut to love's life potential — that is not the way God loves. For married love (or any love) to be authentic, it must be an instance of that total, no-strings-attached, fully accepting way God treasures his chosen.

The other sign for special commitment is Ordination. Priesthood is one of the Lord's exercises in creation — creating something from nothing. God often reminded the tribe of Israel that they were "nobodies" before he chose them. Likewise, no one really qualifies to "take this honor on his own initiative, but only when called by God . . . ." This same unknown author of Hebrews asserts that "every high priest is taken from among men and made their representative before God to offer gifts and sacrifices for sins." A priest is one of the Christian crowd who, to his surprise, hears that he has been singled out. He is, though, singled out as Christ was — for the purpose of sacrifice (worship) of the Father. As one from the crowd he should be all too conscious of the frail, flawed people he comes from, and especially conscious of his own moral frailty. "He is able to deal patiently with erring sinners, for he himself is beset by weakness and so must make sin offerings for himself as well as for the people" (Hebrews 5:2-3).

Ordination is a beckoning by God to enter his Holy of Holies, but it does not create saints. As with all the sacraments, God waits upon us to try on the grace of the sacrament and make it our own. I remember the story a woman told of her Catholic grade school experience with Sisters in full habit. She said she ran home from school one day shouting to her mother, "They have feet! They have feet!" She had presumed that a religious glided above the floor by some angelic locomotion. A peek at an ankle quickly disavowed her of that notion. Priests likewise have feet, and often enough, as *Hebrews* warns us, feet of clay.

A priest, like every Christian, is invited to be a saint according to the goal of his mission. That mission, as in marriage, is a call to service in a community. A barber once asked me, "What on earth do you do after saying Mass in the morning?" The servant-priest does preside over community worship and is to be communal voice and hand when need be. He is to bear so striking a resemblance to Jesus that he can even say Jesus' words of offering, forgiving, or healing with an identical effect. But "after saying Mass in the morning" and other rituals, he is cut out to understand his people. "He is able to deal patiently with erring sinners, for he himself is beset by weakness." Surveys and questionnaires reveal that this is precisely what the community of Christ wants — not so much a genius, or even a saint, but someone who can emphathize with problems and weaknesses. It seems that God's people need a priest who is a human being on their own wavelength. How ironic and contrary to standard expectations that priestly ordination should make the person more thoroughly human, or shall we say humane. But, after all, isn't that holiness — our being exactly what God made us for others?

Anyone married or ordained is a model moving after the fashion of Jesus. He was that person totally for others. He "entered into his glory" precisely because he "loved the Church and gave himself for it." What, we might ask, of the many who love and give of themselves, but seemingly have no sacrament specially geared for their missions, be they religious Sisters or single men and women? Much more needs to be thought out on the theology of the single life. A Tom Dooley or a Dorothy Day need not feel unchosen or noncommissioned. The Spirit is there all the while chipping away to verify that likeness of the Father we have in Jesus. It is not that we have to fall back on Baptism, Confirmation, and the Eucharist for a rationale of the lay Christian life; the truth is, we have not fully valued the Spirit power of these initial sacraments already creatively at work.

Healed in Root and Branch

The man in the street of Jesus' time saw evil all of a piece; human malice, destructive storms, hunger, mental illness, disease, and death were all one — the disorder wrought by evil. When the crowds witnessed Jesus of Nazareth forgiving sins, calming seas, feeding the hungry, healing the insane and the lepers, raising the dead, they knew that Satan's kingdom was under full-scale attack by God's healing forces. In Jesus, God was evidently making well and whole a sick cosmos. The bystanders might have recalled Yahweh's description of himself during the Exodus sojourn as "your healer." All the sacraments have a hand at mending the pieces of a broken world. Two signs in particular speak of Christ's continued healing ministry, the sacraments of Reconciliation and the Anointing of the Sick.

Rather than pockmarking souls, as we liked to imagine, sin attacks or even unhinges relationships, our relation with our self, our fellow-man, and our God. Moral evil is cancer of the connective tissues. Just so, the sign of Reconciliation turns Christians back in touch with themselves, with one another, and with their Maker. God's forgiveness in the sacrament is not simply a cosmetic repair job; it is truly rehabilitating, reconciling. His absolution is completely therapeutic so that our turnaround is a full 180 degrees.

I once saw two workers taking a coffee break. One of them had a way of constantly teasing the other. This day the teasing went too far and an angry outburst resulted. The bitter feeling parted the two to opposite ends of the building. After a while a mutual friend of theirs went looking for both antagonists to bring them together and to settle their differences. In the process he insisted that they shake hands as a sign of their fully renewed friendship. Now that is what Christ effects in the sacrament of Reconciliation. Reconciling is a complete healing of the division, the estrangement we all experience within ourselves, from our neighbor, and from our God. A celebration of reconciliation is at the core of Vatican II's renewal of Penance. This refurbishing is much more than a change of ritual; it is a restoring appreciation of God's healing power. In the Biblical sense of "repentance," it brings us from an awareness of sin's corrosive force and then turns us around to a thorough healing of friendships. This reconciling sacrament celebrates the hand-in-hand clasping of friends rejoined one to another.

Many who believe in their Father's ready forgiveness have difficulty with the confession of sins. "Why must I tell my sins to a man to obtain God's forgiveness?" (This question does, in a sense, pick an argument with the Lord's preferred style of operating.) There are, of course, other channels of forgiveness available, such as private appeal to his mercy and the charity that "covers a multitude of sins." Yet, our transgressions are seldom completely private since they usually somehow tread on the toes of our community members. It is only appropriate, then, that we are reconciled to the community we have wounded, or to one official representative member at least. Absolution was early thought of as a second Baptism in the case of a Christian who had pruned himself off from the communal vine. Reconciliation was then, like Baptism, a professional regrafting onto Christ's vine and branch.

Probably the most efficacious act of any penitent is getting down on his knees (really, or at least psychologically) to voice before God and one other community member his self-accusation — "I'm a sinner." There is not only the therapeutic value of speaking the name of the beast but also the total assurance that he has actually heard Jesus say, "Your sins are forgiven." It is one thing to affirm the Creed's "I believe in the forgiveness of sins"; it is quite another matter to hear and experience that forgiveness.

We should come to an experience of the Father's mercy with the attitude that he is more eager to forgive than we are to be forgiven. The father of the prodigal son (see Luke 15:11-32) is our God and Father: "While he was still a long way off his father caught sight of him and was deeply moved. He ran out to meet him, threw his arms around his neck, and kissed him." At the beginning of the renewed Penance ritual, there is a greeting by the priest reminding us of the Father's readiness to reconcile. For instance, from Psalm 103:

Bless the Lord, O my soul,
and forget not all his benefits;

He pardons all your iniquities,
   he heals all your ills.
He redeems your life from destruction,
   he crowns you with kindness and compassion,
He fills your lifetime with good;
   your youth is renewed like the eagle's.

It is also hoped that we come to reconciliation with a deeper understanding of our failures. Sin is not merely an act, but the interior attitude which prompts the act. One very discerning definition of sin speaks of a "willingness to let my relationship with God be strained, or even broken." The offense stems from our disposition to be apart and alone, at odds with our Creator and his human community. Even though, for example, the sinner may have gone along with the peer pressure of a group, he or she is opting for isolation or even exile.

The present option of conference-style confession will hopefully enable us to tear up the laundry list recitation of sins and will encourage an understanding of the patterns of evil that occur in our lives. An overall profile of guilt should focus on our more basic flaws at the very heart of darkness. Discussing our "warts and all" should lead to an awareness of the social structures of sin built into and even assumed in our culture. There is the theory that original sin may well be the personal and social brokenness we are both into and blithely perpetuate. A discussion of the social dimension of our behavior may even successfully attack the split personality between our religious life and our real life.

Reconciliation, then, is the rediscovery of unity and integrity, a putting back together what should be whole. Its healing of our brokenness as well as its reintegration into community is nicely illustrated by clasped hands. In fact, Yahweh's always outstretched hand is the Old Testament sign of his available mercy. Isaiah has God pleading:

I was ready to respond to those who asked me not, to be found by those who sought me not. I said: Here I am! Here I am! . . . I have stretched out my hands all the day to a rebellious people (Isaiah 65:1-2).

The Press of the Crowd

We are shattered and sundered in so many ways, and not the least are the ills of mind and body. Jesus was second to none in his concern for the mentally and physically disabled. So widespread was his reputation for healing of this sort that, as soon as word spread of Jesus' entering a village, seemingly the entire population was at his doorstep for relief of maladies. St. Mark regularly concludes episodes of the Lord's public mission by a summary account of mass cures:

The crowds scurried about the adjacent area and began to bring in sick on bedrolls to the place where they heard he was. Wherever he put in an appearance, in villages, in towns, or at crossroads, they laid the sick in the maket places and begged him to let them touch just the tassel of his cloak. All who touched him got well (Mark 6:55-56).

On occasion the press of the crowd in need of remedy was such that Jesus and his disciples could not even find time or opportunity to eat! To meet the demand, Jesus sent the Twelve out in pairs on healing missions of their own. "They expelled many demons, anointed the sick with oil, and worked many cures." One has only to attend a communal healing of the sick to realize the still extensive need for Christ's curative touch. No Church service for the Anointing of the Sick is ever canceled for the lack of patients; quite the contrary, the same long lines as in Biblical times keep pressing forward. The prevalence of mind and body ills still speaks of our brokenness. (It is the rare person even today who can say, "I have never had a sick day in my life.") The lame and the blind still come, and Christ still heals!

All of the sacraments have undergone some retooling since Vatican II, but none so radically and successfully as the Anointing of the Sick. We are reminded that the classical text for the Church's healing practice always did speak of health, rather than possible death, as indicated in the phrase "the Last Rites." "This prayer uttered in faith will reclaim the one who is ill, and the Lord will restore him to health." The Catholic community needed little urging by the Council to respond to Christ's sick call, for the "crowds scurried . . . to the place where they heard he was." That meeting place is now the healing sacrament. The commentary from James likewise confides that in the Anointing of the Sick "if he has committed any sins, forgiveness will be his." Like the good family doctor, Jesus attends to the whole person, body and spirit.

"But this is faith healing!" some might object. If this is healing by faith in Jesus' power to undo all man's ills, then make the most of it. It is, after all, God who describes himself as "your healer." We know from the Gospels that this healing is very much dependent on faith. Trust in God is the measure of Jesus' healing. Yet, before we cancel that appointment with our doctor and throw away all our pills, we should take the medical advice of Sirach, Chapter 38, verse 2: "From God the doctor has his wisdom." Why does faith in healing have to be the dilemma between the doctor and the Deity? Why not both? We should find ourselves a medical man who is gifted by God and yet knows enough to refer us also to the Healer. We should seek out a physician who prayerfully ministers instead of practices.

How ironic it is that the romantic phrase "divine Physician" has taken on new depth of meaning in the sacraments of Reconciliation and the Anointing of the Sick. We are now more aware that Jesus does not move among us to save disembodied souls, but rather to heal us root and branch, soul and body.

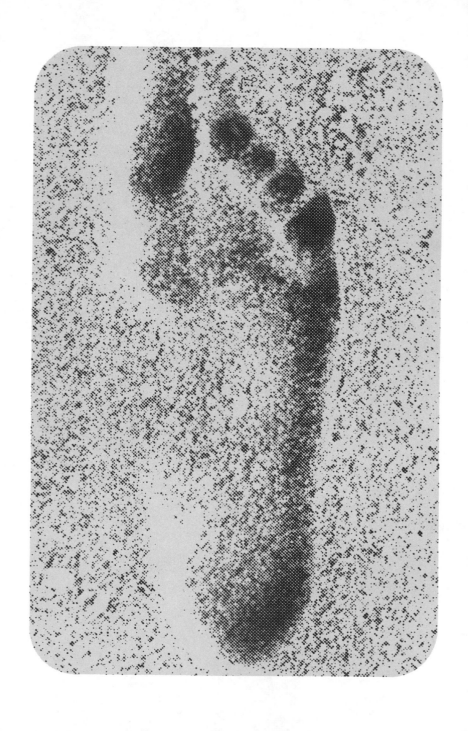

X
Your Journey in the Spirit

In the great prayer that concludes the Last Supper discourse, Jesus underscores the tension point at which the Christian must live: "O Father . . . I do not ask you to take them out of the world, but to guard them from the evil one. They are not of the world, any more than I belong to the world" (Jn 17:11, 15-16). We are in the world without belonging; that very much makes us resident aliens — a sticky situation at best. This tenuous residency is molded after the experience of Abraham and the Patriarchs. They lived in exile among alien peoples without truly belonging, residing in God alone, with him as their only stronghold. Our origins too are elsewhere. The Sabbath and the exchange of kinship blood in the Eucharist are both continuing Covenant reminders that we, like them, do not belong. This is because by the Covenant commitment we are not our own. By mutual agreement, we are exclusively God's people, as he is our God. In the new priestly kingdom, we are all clergy, for, as the root of the word "clergy" indicates, we have thrown in our "lot" with the Lord so that he is our "portion." So, the Christian has literally pulled up stakes and journeyed after God as his sole patrimony.

The essential danger to the Covenant is the same one encountered by Israel after the Exodus — to speak as God's people while continuing to live as Pharaoh's. This is the temptation to reassert one's self by encroaching, by poaching God's domain, and perhaps setting up a counter-rule by "becoming as gods," reminiscent of Eden. In the process of maturing so many mistake being their own man with being themselves. The Christian, though, has a new "self." "Whoever is joined to the Lord becomes one spirit with him." Indeed, the disciples of Jesus do not belong, not even to themselves.

Christ does tell his followers to count the cost beforehand: There is no other way to come after him than to "die to self." "Whoever would save his life will lose it, but whoever loses his life for my sake will find it." To be a son or a daughter of the heavenly Father means hearing his word, dutifully working out his will, being his living, even crucified image.

Yet, every cell of our being cries out in fear of extinction. The instinct for self-preservation sounds the fearful alarm! Ah, but do not confuse absorption with extinction. There is no dissolution of self, for it is only in letting go that we find our true self. "He who seeks only himself brings himself to ruin, whereas he who brings himself to nought for me discovers who he is." It is only in being absorbed into an infinitely better "Self" that we become identifiably alive. We discover our identity by coming to know ourselves in relationship and in the context of our origins. By getting out of ourselves we uncover the mystery of our birth, that we are "born of God." We are, as we find in the Jewish Scriptures, the apple of our Father's eye. In this light and in response to our fears of extinction, Jesus chides, "Why are you so fearful? Trust in God and trust in me." After all, would our Father and life-giver let his own line become extinct?

Safari of the Spirit

The agenda for Christian life is easily capsulized in the bumper sticker slogan "Let Go and Let God." What the Savior demands of his disciples is ordinarily well beyond them. Since the new person asserting himself is the risen Christ, it will then have to be his doing. "We are Christ's and Christ is God's"; so nothing is impossible. And it is so much simpler a way of life to allow the Almighty to meet our crises, solve our dilemmas, or achieve what for us is unlikely — in his own paradoxical way. Bumper sticker philosophy is often humorous and sometimes nonsense, but "Let Go and Let God" is right on the bumper!

"Letting God" likewise holds out the lure of adventure. God's pace and style of moving is delightfully different. Each day, then, offers adventure for those who delight in his ironic, yet exquisite pattern of operation. With a sense of expectation we can wonder, "What person will God have me meet today?" or "What needs will Jesus, living in me, reach out and touch this day?" Often the way the Lord sorts out and arranges things is a marvel to behold. We, too, can expect to acclaim that Jesus "has done all things well." Yet, this open-ended adventure is only for those who refrain from planning their own agendas and "Let God." What is the use of being possessed by the Spirit's power unless that delightful dynamism is free to "blow where it will"? The ultimate safari is the journey led by the Spirit.

Surely, though, we have some choices, some decisions to make on our own. The self is not extinguished. Unlike a mere mirror image, the Christian self decides and even loves to reflect the Spirit "blowing where it will." One of the fine spiritual arts is sensing which way the Spirit blows. I say "sensing" because included in the equipment given for our expedition is the gift of discernment — a part of the travel pack called the gifts of the Spirit. Discernment is the sense or instinct for knowing what is God's pattern of moving and what is not. This art of reading the direction of God's breeze, rather than our own, is shaped by Baptism and fine-honed by Confirmation. We soon learn the sense of rightness, the feel of God's own peace in moving his due way. Fear not, the Lord is both power as well as pilot for this excursion.

Just how the Christian travels is a matter of class. The pilgrimage with Jesus to our Father is choice indeed. Still, traveling first-class in the Gospel sense of the journey means going last (the perfect irony of "the last shall be first"). There are not too many people taking the last places these days, so there is at least far less hubbub to the rear. For absolute luxury-class we sign on board as stewards — "the greatest among you is the one who serves." That, after all, is how Jesus traveled in our midst. "He emptied himself and took the form of a slave."

Upstairs, Downstairs would have said that Christ was "in service," a fulfillment of Isaiah's prophecy that the Savior would be his Father's best servant. Because he so often recited it, an observant Jew like Jesus was always reminded that the first and greatest commandment was to "Serve the Lord, your God" with a totality of being — heart, soul, and mind. This is precisely Jesus' great accomplishment and his glory. "Because of this, God highly exalted him and bestowed on him the name above every other name" (Phil 2:9). There is no other way to enter upstairs into his glory except by "going into service" through the downstairs door. This, of course, is not service isolated to God alone, but to a Creator who is very much aligned with his creation. "Whatever you do to the least" is service to him.

The Gift to be Simple

The Christian should travel in style, that is, simply and simply for God. On sending his disciples out on missions of service, Jesus is quite explicit that they take a few encumbrances to weigh themselves down. Only the bare necessities and no extras is the weight limit. They traveled with faith that the Father was to be their faithful supply master; so no need to overstock. The modern disciple will have to decide for him or herself what is necessary and what is extra. In any case, we are called to simplify our life style. Freedom from the burden and clutter of things gives greater freedom for service, as well as freedom for mobility and daring. It is always well on occasion to look around and check whether we are possibly possessed by this or that thing. We might ask ourselves, "Would I be crushed if this object were lost to me?" We should try once in a while to test our detachment by taking a prized treasure and passing it on to a friend in need or to some charity that would prize it more. "One thing only is needful." The style of Christianity is simplicity itself.

It is not sufficient, however, to live simply; a disciple of Jesus is also committed to living simply for God. Not only does he or she "serve the Lord, our God," but "him only shall you serve." This service is exclusive, if not jealously guarded. "No man can serve two masters. . . . You cannot give yourself to God and money. . . . Your heavenly Father knows all that you need. Seek first his kingship over you, his way of holiness, and all these things will be given you besides" (Matthew 16:24, 32-33). In real-life terms this means giving our God the first fruits of our time, our labor, our money, rather than the usual hindmost. Do we come before him bearing offerings of leftovers? If the single-hearted of the beatitudes are looking for a bumper sticker slogan, they could well dip into the wisdom of the Psalms. Psalm 62 poses in prayer the ideal attitude of exclusive trust: "Only in God be at rest, my soul, for from him comes my hope." Still, the only way to experience for ourselves that "one thing only is needful" and that "all will be given you besides" is to try it. The Father is faithful and only asks for a similar fidelity so that he might lavish upon us exactly what we need.

The Lord is waiting to show you favor . . . . He will be gracious to you when you cry out, as soon as he hears he will answer you. The Lord will give you the bread you need and the water for which you thirst (Isaiah 30:18-20). This also presumes that the Father can read the real needs of his children better than they themselves can. But what is a Father for if not to be provident for his own! The tribe of Israel, in the desert experience, found that their God easily provided the necessities in a wasteland, if they sought and followed him only. Even a gourmet banquet of quail was flown in at their request. Divine care goes well beyond the bare bones of necessity to the creation of treats, usually when least expected. Yahweh is very capable of surprise. Waiting upon his delights is also part of the adventure of moving with God.

Traveler's Aid

Some feel insecure unless all the dos and don'ts are spelled out for them. In actual practice any who follow Christ are ultimately thrown back upon the moral judgment we call their conscience. Conscience is not a "little voice" or the good angel saying "now, now!" It is, rather, the Christian, who draws upon the resources of the Gospel message held in the hand of the Church, judging what is appropriate in his context. No one else can rightly assume to judge that this or that particular relationship mirrors God's love or is a warped imitation of it. Those who avoid taking this mature responsibility upon themselves drift to the extremes of either a lax or a scrupulous conscience — for them, mostly everything is pretty much all right or everything is sinful.

But, for those who take courage in hand to be responsible for their own actions, there is the assurance that their Father has faith in them — he trusts and abides by their honest judgments. It is reassuring to have a Father who relies on his offspring to make these kinds of decisions. (Like any good father, he exudes such a loving acceptance that we even have the courage to look our failings straight in the eye and to keep going with the guarantee that we are most acceptable.) Then too, we always have our sixth sense, the instinct of the Spirit, as a friendly and wiser companion along the way.

"The way," as the Acts of the Apostles calls the Christian life, is a lived experience and not an academic debate. Moses was the first of many to warn against the danger of talking religion, rather than "heeding" the Lord's voice and "keeping" his commandments. The final advice by Moses to the Israelite nation points out that God's command is not mysterious and remote, but clearly at hand to be implemented:

It is not up in the sky, that you should say, 'Who will go up in the sky to get it for us and tell us of it, that we may carry it out?' Nor is it across the sea, that we should say, 'Who will cross the sea to get it for us and tell us of it, that we may carry it out?' No, it is something very near to you, already in your mouths and in your hearts; you have only to carry it out (Deuteronomy 30:12-14).

Jesus, in the same vein, faulted the Pharisees of his day because they more often argued the subtleties of God's Word instead of doing the will of their Father. They were more occupied asking questions rather than doing the good lying at their very feet. The "legal eagles" of the Jewish community were forever asking queries, such as "Which commandment of the law is the greatest?" and "Who is my neighbor?" Christ answers that the First Commandment is obviously the first! What's to argue? *"Do this and you shall live."* The parable of the Good Samaritan depicts a dire need lying in the road waiting to be picked up. This vignette of a mugging, given to illustrate a love like God's in motion, concludes with the mandate, "Go and *do* the same." Love is not just something we talk about, it is something we do. It is the "doers" and not the debaters who are as intimately related to Jesus as "brother, and sister, and mother."

If we want some practical advice for "doing the will of our heavenly Father," we might take along some Old Testament nourishing for the mouth and the heart. Jesus, after all, grew up on the Jewish Bible, made it his own, and incorporated it into his words and deeds. The Wisdom portion of the Hebrew Scriptures is his special favorite. From the Wisdom literature, Psalm 15 is a pointed, practical application of the social virtues:

O Lord, who shall sojourn in your tent?
Who shall dwell on your holy mountain?
He who walks blamelessly and does justice;
who thinks the truth in his heart
and slanders not with his tongue;
Who harms not his fellow man,
nor takes up a reproach against his neighbor;
By whom the reprobate is despised,
while he honors those who fear the Lord;
Who, though it be to his loss, changes
not his pledged word;
who lends not his money at usury
and accepts no bribe against the innocent.
He who does these things shall never be disturbed.

The Book of Tobit is a parable about faith, even in time of adversity. The story centers around a journey. One chapter is reminiscent of Polonius' advice to his son in *Hamlet;* Tobit, before his son travels afar, gives him words of wisdom:

Through all your days, my son, keep the Lord in mind . . . .
Give alms from your possessions. Do not turn your face away
from any of the poor, and God's face will not be turned away
from you . . . . Do not keep with you overnight the wages of
any man who works for you, but pay him immediately. If you
thus behave as God's servant, you will receive your reward
. . . . Do to no one what you yourself dislike . . . . Give to the
hungry some of your bread, and to the naked some of your
clothing. Whatever you have left over, give away as alms; and
do not begrudge the alms you give . . . . Seek counsel from
every wise man, and do not think lightly of any advice that can
be useful. At all times bless the Lord God, and ask him to
make all your paths straight and to grant success to all your
endeavors and plans (Tobit, chapter 4).

And like the son of Tobit, we too have a heavenly companion for the journey; we have the very Spirit of wisdom. Yahweh assures us, as he did Moses on the trek through the wilderness, "I myself will go along, to give you rest."

XI
Prayer:
Your Life Line
to God

There is a mystical technique from the mysterious East known seemingly to only a few. It has been handed down by generations of devotees to our present day. Through it we can be in touch with the ultimate and possess cosmic power unknown to others. It is called PRAYER. If we wish, we can even use our own mantra (a mystic word to help one focus contemplation). How strange that we are so taken with Eastern cults and their techniques, when all the while we have an open life line to God in prayer. Oriental insights from Zen and the like have much to tell us about prayer, but they are not substitutes for it.

Some pray only in case of emergency. IN CASE OF FIRE BREAK GLASS. Others use it simply to requisition needs, when all the while they should be desiring to learn God's will and share it. Jesus does encourage us to ask our real needs of the Father, but we find that his own prayer life embraces so much more. Prayer is the air Christ breathes. The Lord Jesus could apparently have given himself to so many more valuable pursuits, but instead he is found praying. Rather than cultivate his enthusiastic following, Christ, as Luke notes, "often retired to deserted places and prayed." Luke's Gospel especially pictures Jesus as the man of prayer. He will not be caught up in the heresy of activity, that is, action unsupported by prayer. It is seemingly the battery that keeps the Galilean going. (We can eavesdrop on this life line between Jesus and his Father by reading the so-called High Priestly Prayer in chapter 17 of John's Gospel.)

It follows that anyone who would live the Christ-life without time for personal prayer is like an astronaut walking in space without an umbilical — he has no invisible means of life support. Husbands and wives, for instance, who avoid being alone with each other are strange spouses indeed. It is said that we waste time on what we truly prize. Granted that prayer takes time when so many tasks demand our time, yet it is the one "extravagance" the Christian must afford. Without it, anemia or even death of the Spirit ensues.

It is curious how few followers of Christ consider themselves equipped, much less adept at prayer! Maybe it is because they have so little to say aside from asking for basic needs. That, however, is a near-sighted viewpoint of prayer life. It is not so much what we have to say to God, but what God has to say to us! We often address God as we would a deaf, mute child who can only nod "yes" or "no." We should expect, instead, that God really wants to lead us in prayer, to tell us about himself and about ourselves (yes, we come to discover who we are before God). If we have high expectations that Jesus' Spirit will touch our thoughts, our imagination, our feelings, it will happen. We must begin to pray with faith that the Father wants to be in dialogue with us. So often we talk God's ear off, when all the while he has so much to say to us. Think of prayer, then, as a meeting of Father and child, or Jesus and friend — a communion of family members who have much in common to share. In that vein, we would love to "waste time" on God.

The enemy of a rich prayer life is a feeling of self-sufficiency. Some of Jesus' contemporaries felt all too smug and complacent in God's favor. They bragged, "Abraham is our father"— their family had the monopoly on religion. To this attitude John the Baptizer gave the perfect rebuttal. "I tell you, God can raise up children to Abraham from these very stones." Anyone who has been to Israel knows that stones are its most plentiful natural resource. John is simply saying that God could, if he wished, take the most common, basic element and create a people of his own. There is no reason for smug complacency. A special relationship with God is something we could never earn, and, once we are related, never deserve. It is sheer gift due in no way to our own worth or efforts. For that reason we speak of the Father's relationship to us as "grace" — as absolute favor. We have no reason to be proud, no more than a rock or a stone. It is the Father who has chosen us for his own inexplicable reasons. To his gracious invitation, "Live in my love," we can only respond in prayerful gratitude.

St. Ignatius Loyola was accustomed to making his morning offering, "Lord, what can I do for you today?" A generous prayer, but let me take issue with it. It is not primarily a matter of what we can do for God, but what he can do for us. He is the one choosing and giving. I should think a more appropriate morning prayer is one of responsive acceptance, something like "Lord, what marvelous thing you are going to do for me this day! I accept from your hands all that you give me for my good, all that you take away for my good. Everything is your gift. I thank you, Father, for this day with the gift of your Spirit alive in me."

There are many ways of praying, either privately or sharing in common, by the use of formal prayer texts or in silence, by informal conversation or with passive receptivity. Whatever works is best. Even then, effective styles of prayer for any one person will vary from time to time. As in marriage, the relationship should progress and mature. Expectedly, the Spirit of God will move in and take a more active role as we let him.

Transcendental meditation may have something useful to say about initiating prayer. As with TM, this is ideally practiced twice a day for about 15 or 20 minutes (preferably, however, not after a full meal). Choose a quiet spot if possible and sit, your back straight, but your body very relaxed. To begin with, try several deep breaths and completely relax on the exhale. To quiet down your thoughts and to exclude distractions, use a mantra, the repeated word "Jesus" or "Father," to the rhythm of your breathing. These names of God invoke his presence and evoke his love in which you live and breathe.

Some guidelines as you pray:

1) Prayer is not necessarily to be confused with talking. As one's prayer life matures, it should usually become more wordless. If you have something to talk over with God, fine, but otherwise think the mantra slowly to yourself. This word, though, is simply a device for focusing your relationship with God; after a while you will want to dispense with it and be still, just aware and appreciative of your being in God's presence. It is enough that God is and you are, and you are bound to him in a life-giving kinship — like the vine and its branch. It is sufficient to BE with your Father.

2) Do not try too hard. Do not be anxious how you are to pray or how your prayer is going. Relax! God moves as and when he will.

3) If distractions intrude, as they will, use the mantra for a while to refocus upon God.
4) By this time you are becoming anxious whether things are working as they should. Nothing seems to be happening. You have conceived no great or holy thoughts! RELAX. Make no mind — you have to become nothing so that God can become all in all. Just wait upon the Lord. He is in charge; in essence it is his prayer to do with as he wills.
5) Have faith that God really wants to guide your thoughts, to tell you about himself and yourself. It is his Spirit who prays in you.
6) Be real with God and with yourself. At prayer you are most real for once.
7) Lastly, there is no substitute for actual practice. You learn to pray by praying.

It is all a matter of priority. Your best offering to the Father through Jesus may be the gift of your precious time. Some activists might call prayer spendthrift, but those who lavish and waste time on the Lord are the real movers of this globe. "More things are wrought by prayer than this world dreams of."